ALL-COLOUR COOKBOOK

*I dedicate this book to Mother Martie —
my mother and my best friend!*

ALL-COLOUR COOKBOOK

PHOTOGRAPHY BY CHRIS WAGNER

STRUIK

Struik Publishers (Pty) Ltd
(a member of The Struik Publishing Group (Pty) Ltd)
Cornelis Struik House
80 McKenzie Street
Cape Town 8001

Reg. No.: 54/00965/07

First edition August 1994
Second impression December 1994

Text and photographs © Annette Human 1994

Editor Thea Coetzee
Translator Sylvia Grobbelaar
Designer Janice Evans
Cover design Lauren Mendelson
DTP make-up Struik DTP
Typesetting Lauren Mendelson
Colour developing by Ronald Lewis, Pretoria
Reproduction by Hirt & Carter (Pty) Ltd, Cape Town
Printed and bound by Cape & Transvaal Printers (Pty) Ltd, Cape Town

ISBN 1 86825 616 2

All rights reserved. No part of this publication
may be reproduced, stored in a retrieval system
or transmitted in any form or by any means, electronic,
mechanical, photocopying, recording or otherwise,
without the written permission of the copyright owner.

Translated from *Raakvat-resepte* of 1994

CONTENTS

Foreword **7**

Soup **8**

Vegetables **18**

Salad **28**

Fish **38**

Meat **48**

Light Meals **66**

Puddings **72**

Tarts **86**

Cakes **96**

Small Cakes and Biscuits **106**

Vetkoek, Scones and Muffins **122**

Bread and Rolls **136**

Rusks **152**

Index **158**

FOREWORD

Good advice given a hundred years ago is still as valid today. In December 1890 Miss E.J. Dijkman wrote these words, roughly translated, in the foreword of her recipe book *Di Suid Afrikaanse kook-, koek- en resepte boek*, the first printed Afrikaans cookery book: 'If you weigh (the ingredients) carefully and follow the recipes to the letter, then everything will be a success. It will be your own fault if it doesn't turn out well. So, take note and weigh and measure everything carefully, even if it means going to a bit of trouble. The result will justify the trouble you take, believe me, as I know from experience.'

Elizabeth June Dijkman's maiden name was Eckley and she was born in London. Only after she married Dijkman, the missionary from Paarl, did she seriously make a point of learning Afrikaans and the Afrikaans cuisine.

I agree with her words written a hundred years ago. Every recipe in *All-Colour Cookbook* will be a great success if the ingredients are weighed or measured precisely and the method followed exactly.

Because the capacity of measuring utensils varies so much, you should make sure that for the recipes in this book you only use a measuring cup with a volume of 250 ml, a tablespoon with a volume of 15 ml (not 12,5 ml!) and a teaspoon with a volume of 5 ml.

The flour is measured unsifted throughout. If you prefer to measure it in cups, you should use a scoop or a large spoon to dish it out of the container into the measuring cup, and then level the contents. Don't dish from the container with the measuring cup itself.

Don't use eggs that have just been taken from the refrigerator. Leave them to stand for a while at room temperature.

The abbreviations used are:

c = cup
T = tablespoon
t = teaspoon

All the recipes in *All-Colour Cookbook* are favourites of my family, my relatives and my friends. Enjoy them with us!

Hoogland
March 1994

SOUP

There are days in winter, and even in summer, when there could be nothing better than a plate of steaming soup and a slice of fresh bread, with just butter on it. A pot of soup is a nourishing meal, is never a flop and pleases everybody. In addition, it's ideal for busy people with little time for cooking, because you can make a large quantity in one go and freeze it in meal-sized portions.

NOURISHING VEGETABLE SOUP

This soup sticks to the ribs. It's a meal on its own and freezes well. Store dry soup mix in the freezer to keep mites away.

    180 g soup mix of lentils, oats, barley and peas (1 c)
    4 litres water (16 c)
    4 pieces shin with marrow
    2 large carrots
    2 large potatoes
    1 large onion
    1 tin (410 g) whole peeled tomatoes
    100 g chopped celery (1 c)
    100 g broken spaghetti (1 c)
    25 ml salt (5 t)
    20 ml Worcestershire sauce (4 t)
    1 ml curry powder (¼ t)
    pinch of pepper
    finely chopped parsley

Soak the soup mix in the water for an hour or so. Add the soup meat and cook it until tender. Spoon out the meat.

Peel the carrots and grate coarsely. Peel and halve the potatoes. Peel and chop the onion. Cut up the tomatoes. Add the carrots, potatoes, onions, tomatoes with their juice and the celery to the soup mix and boil until the potatoes are soft.

Remove the potatoes from the soup and add the spaghetti, salt, Worcestershire sauce, curry powder and pepper. Boil until the spaghetti is done.

Mash the potatoes. Cut up the soup meat and add, together with the mashed potatoes, to the soup. Boil till it is well blended. Sprinkle the soup with a little parsley and serve hot.

Makes 4 litres (16 c) soup

FRIED BREAD

These pieces of crisply fried bread are good with a steaming bowl of soup in winter.

    slices of white bread
    sunflower oil
    coarsely grated Cheddar cheese
    salt and pepper
    chopped fresh herbs

Halve the slices of bread and fry in moderately hot, shallow oil in a frying pan till golden brown on the bottom. Turn, sprinkle with a little cheese and fry lightly until the cheese melts. Drain on paper towels, season lightly with salt and pepper and sprinkle with chopped, fresh herbs. Serve immediately.

SOUP 9

QUICK HEALTH SOUP

When we've been eating too much rich food and want to mend our ways a little, this soup is just the right thing to eat the next day. It tastes good and freezes well.

- 1 medium cabbage
- 1 bunch salad celery
- 6 medium onions
- 2 large, ripe tomatoes
- 2 medium green peppers
- 5 litres boiling water (20 c)
- 1 packet brown onion soup powder
- 30 ml finely chopped parsley (2 T)
- 15 ml salt (1 T)
- 1 ml pepper (¼ t)

Shred the cabbage and celery. Peel the onions and tomatoes and chop roughly. Halve and seed the peppers and cut into strips. Put all the prepared vegetables into a large saucepan. Add the boiling water, soup powder, parsley, salt and pepper and stir until well blended.

Bring the mixture to the boil and cook the soup for exactly 10 minutes. Allow the soup to cool very quickly.

Makes 5 litres (20 c) soup

A ONE-WEEK DIET

Eat as much Quick Health Soup as you like every day, as well as the following:

Day 1: Any fruit, especially watermelon and sweet melon, but no bananas.

Day 2: Any vegetables, with the exception of beans, mealies and peas.

Day 3: Any fruit and vegetables, with the exception of bananas and potatoes.

Day 4: Up to 8 bananas and no more than 8 glasses of milk.

Day 5: Up to 350 g lean beef and 6 tomatoes plus 8 glasses of water.

Day 6: As much lean beef and vegetables as you want, except potatoes.

Day 7: As much brown rice, vegetables, fruit and fruit juice as you want.

POTATO SOUP

You may substitute a leek for the onion in this recipe. The soup looks most attractive when garnished just before serving with fresh, chopped herbs such as parsley, chives or dill. It is delicious with crusty, sesame-topped bread rolls.

The best potato cultivar to use in making soup is 'Up-to-date', because it disintegrates quite easily. If it is unobtainable, 'BP1' is a good substitute. Don't use 'Vanderplank' potatoes for making potato soup – this cultivar is actually better for making potato chips.

    750 g marrow bones with meat
    15 ml salt (1 T)
    1 ml pepper (¼ t)
    1 kg potatoes
    1 large onion
    1 large carrot
    250 g shredded celery (2 c)
    50 g butter/margarine (4 T)
    30 ml sunflower oil (2 T)

Season the shin with salt and pepper. Cover with boiling water and cook until the meat comes away from the bones. Remove the meat and marrow and discard the bones. Add enough boiling water to this meat stock to make 2 litres (8 c).

Peel the potatoes, onion and carrot. Dice the potatoes, roughly chop the onion and grate the carrot. Add the celery to the prepared vegetables.

Sauté the potatoes, onion, carrot and celery in the butter/margarine and oil. Add the meat stock and boil, covered, until the potatoes are tender. Mash gently.

Cut up the meat, add it to the soup together with the marrow and bring to the boil. Serve the soup hot.

Makes 3,25 litres (13 c) soup

12 SOUP

BEAN SOUP WITH BUTTERMILK DUMPLINGS

When the Cape wind howls around the corner of our West Coast cottage and the waves seem intent on smashing the rocks, I make sure that there's a pot of bean soup simmering away on the stove. When the day is miserable and the cold has set in, what could be more cheering than a good pot of bean soup with light-as-air dumplings floating on top?

Cook the soup in a saucepan with a diameter of at least 25 cm, so that there is enough room for all the dumplings to fit on top of the soup.

This is rather a large recipe, but fortunately both the soup and the dumplings freeze very well.

I usually use speckled sugar beans when I make this soup, because I generally have a supply of them in stock, but you may also successfully use haricot or butter beans, although the soup will then be lighter in colour.

Never add salt to dried beans before they are properly cooked and tender. If you add salt at the beginning of the cooking time, the beans won't become soft.

SOUP
500 g speckled sugar beans (2½ c)
1 kg marrow bones with meat
30 ml salt (2 T)
3 bay leaves
5 ml dried thyme (1 t)
2 ml black pepper (½ t)
2 large onions

DUMPLINGS
140 g cake flour (1 c)
5 ml baking powder (1 t)
2 ml salt (½ t)
pinch of pepper
125 ml buttermilk (½ c)
15 ml sunflower oil (1 T)
chopped parsley/spring onions

Spread out the sugar beans on a table and remove all the impurities. Cover the beans with plenty of water and soak overnight. (Alternatively, bring the beans to the boil in plenty of water and cook for about 10 minutes. Remove the saucepan from the heat and leave the beans to soak for approximately 2 hours.)

Drain the soaked beans. Cover with fresh boiling water and cook till soft. The beans should have a floury texture when rubbed between the fingers. (Add a knob of butter/margarine if the water threatens to froth over the edge of the saucepan.)

At the same time, in another saucepan, boil the meat, salt, bay leaves, thyme and black pepper with plenty of water until the meat comes away from the bones.

Measure the meat stock and the water in which the beans were cooked. Add enough boiling water to this liquid to make 3 litres (12 c). Add the cooking liquid to the beans.

Peel and roughly chop the onions. Add to the beans and cook till tender.

Remove the shin bones. Cut up the meat and marrow and add it to the soup. Mash the beans lightly with a potato masher. Leave the soup to simmer while you make the dumplings.

Sift together the flour, baking powder, salt and pepper. Beat the buttermilk and the oil together. Add this mixture to the flour, stirring to make a smooth batter.

Place teaspoons of the batter into the soup. Put on the lid and let the dumplings simmer for 15 minutes.

Ladle the soup and dumplings into a tureen, sprinkle with a little chopped parsley or spring onions and serve hot.

Makes about 4 litres (16 c) soup and 1½ dozen dumplings

MUSHROOM SOUP

This is not only excellent as a soup, but can also be used as a luscious 'pepper' sauce on juicy grilled steaks. For a sauce, halve the recipe, but retain the 2 ml (½ t) curry powder and sprinkle generously with black pepper.

Garnish the soup with a few slices of fried mushroom, a little thick cream and a sprig of parsley.

> 500 g fresh mushrooms
> 75 g butter/margarine (5½ T)
> 2 ml curry powder (½ t)
> 30 g cake flour (3 T)
> 500 ml chicken stock (2 c)
> 1 tin (410 g) evaporated milk
> 5 ml salt (1 t)
> pinch of pepper

Wipe the mushrooms with a damp kitchen towel and slice them. Fry the mushrooms in the butter/margarine, only until they start to draw water.

Add the curry powder to the mushrooms, then stir in the flour and the chicken stock. Allow the mixture to boil for a few minutes.

Purée or blend the mushroom mixture. Lastly, add the evaporated milk, salt and pepper and bring to the boil. Serve hot.

Makes 1,2 litres (5 c) soup

IN THE MICROWAVE OVEN

Use 100% power throughout. Prepare the mushrooms as described in the recipe. Melt the butter/margarine. Stir in the curry powder and microwave for approximately 30 seconds. Add the mushrooms and microwave until soft. Sprinkle the cake flour over the mushrooms and mix well. Add the chicken stock and heat the mixture to boiling point. Purée or blend, add the remaining ingredients and heat the soup through before serving.

BUTTERNUT SOUP

Each bowl of soup may be garnished with a teaspoon of cream and a little finely chopped parsley.

For an interesting variation, replace the nutmeg with a little finely grated orange rind and add a few shreds of orange rind to the garnish.

    2 medium butternut squash
    1 Granny Smith apple
    2 medium onions
    50 g butter/margarine (4 T)
    7 ml medium curry powder (1½ t)
    40 g cake flour (4 T)
    pinch of ground nutmeg
    2 chicken stock cubes
    750 ml boiling water (3 c)
    500 ml milk (2 c)
    7 ml salt (1½ t)

Peel, seed and dice the butternuts. Peel, core and chop the apple. Peel the onions and chop roughly.

In a large saucepan, sauté the chopped onions in the butter/margarine. Add the curry powder and fry the mixture lightly. Add the butternut and apple and sauté the mixture for a while. Add the flour and nutmeg and stir-fry lightly.

Dissolve the chicken stock cubes in the boiling water. Add the stock, together with the milk and salt, to the butternut mixture. Boil, with the lid on, over moderate heat until the butternut pieces are soft. Stir the mixture occasionally.

Purée or blend until smooth. The colour of the soup should be a deep yellow and the texture creamy. Serve the soup hot.

Makes 2 litres (8 c) soup

SOUP 15

MELKSNYSELS (MILK NOODLES)

Whenever melksnysels featured on the menu, my granny, Annie van Jaarsveld, used to spend the late afternoon on the back stoep at Noupoort cutting up noodles on the old wooden table there. I used to love to watch her skill in cutting the dough into the finest possible strips on an inverted soup plate. We usually eat melksnysels with wholewheat bread and butter.

2 extra large eggs
2 ml salt (½ t)
10 ml butter/margarine (2 t)
200 g cake flour (1½ c)
2 litres milk (8 c)
cinnamon sugar

Lightly beat the eggs and salt. Rub the butter/margarine into the cake flour. Add the egg mixture and mix well to form a stiff dough. Knead well until the dough is smooth and elastic.

Roll the dough out very thinly on a floured pastry board. Cut the dough into 5 cm-wide strips. Sprinkle the strips liberally with flour and pile them on top of each other. Shred the strips into very thin noodles with a sharp knife. Shake the noodles to separate.

Bring the milk to the boil in a large heavy-based saucepan. Add the noodles and simmer for about 20 minutes over low heat until thick and done. Stir often.

Ladle the melksnysels into soup plates and sprinkle each serving with cinnamon sugar. Serve the melksnysels hot.

Makes 4–6 servings

NOODLES IN SOUP

Instead of cooking the noodles in milk, they may also be cooked in bean soup or vegetable soup instead of dumplings, spaghetti or macaroni.

CUSTARD MELKKOS

When milk is abundant on the farm in summer, I use full cream milk for this dish, but when there is no milk at all in winter, I make do with powdered skim milk.

This is one of my husband's firm favourites. He says it is much better than the 'yellow porridge' made of water, flour and custard powder that he concocted as a child. He only wishes he could turn the clock back for such a treat as this melkkos.

    200 g sago (1 c)
    2,5 litres milk (10 c)
    2 eggs
    60 ml water (¼ c)
    30 g custard powder (4 T)
    2 ml salt (½ t)
    15 ml butter/margarine (1 T)
    cinnamon sugar

Soak the sago in the milk for about an hour. Gradually bring the mixture to the boil over moderate heat, using a heavy-based saucepan. Stir it quite often in order to prevent burning and simmer until the sago is soft and transparent.

Separate the eggs. Beat together the egg yolks, water, custard powder and salt. Add the custard mixture to the milk mixture and simmer until thick, stirring often. Add the butter/margarine.

Beat the egg whites until stiff but not dry. Stir a little of the stiffly beaten egg white into the hot melkkos until mixed. Then lightly fold the remaining egg white into the mixture, using a metal spoon.

Pour the custard melkkos into a heatproof serving dish, sprinkle lavishly with cinnamon sugar and serve immediately.

Makes 2,5 litres (10 c) melkkos

VEGETABLES

Vegetables form an important part of the daily diet and are so wholesome that we should never neglect them, even though children are so prone to scoff at them. All vegetables – even cabbage and spinach – can taste marvellous if you dress them up, for instance as baked cabbage or spinach fritters. Get to work and stock up the freezer with vegetables when they are abundant and cheap.

GREEN BEAN BAKE

A new way of presenting ordinary green beans is to make them into a savoury filling, to cover them with a tasty potato crust and then to bake.

FILLING
500 g sliced green beans (4 c)
125 g bacon
1 large onion
1 ripe, medium tomato
15 ml cornflour (1 T)
125 ml water (½ c)
5 ml salt (1 t)
pinch of pepper

CRUST
4 medium potatoes
125 ml boiling milk (½ c)
5 ml dried parsley (1 t)
2 ml baking powder (½ t)
2 ml salt (½ t)
pinch of pepper
75 g coarsely grated Cheddar cheese (¾ c)

Cook the beans in the usual way until just done. Drain well.
Chop up the bacon and fry lightly. Peel the onion and tomato and chop roughly. Add to the bacon and fry together for a while. Dissolve the cornflour in the water and add the salt and pepper. Add to the bacon mixture and stir until thickened. Add the green beans and mix. Spoon the mixture into an ovenproof pie dish with a volume of 1,5 litres (6 c).
Peel the potatoes and cut into pieces. Cook in the usual way until soft. Drain and mash. Add the boiling milk, parsley, baking powder, salt and pepper and mix well. Stir in two-thirds of the cheese. Spread the mixture over the filling and sprinkle the remaining cheese on top.
Grill the pie until the crust starts to brown. Serve hot.

Makes 6 servings

BOTTLED GREEN BEANS

Place 2,5 kg shredded green beans in a large enamel saucepan. Add: 250 ml (1 c) white vinegar, 50 g (4 T) sugar, 50 g (3 T) salt and enough boiling water to cover the beans. Boil the beans briskly for exactly 20 minutes without a lid. Spoon the beans into sterilized jars and fill the jars with the vinegar water in which the beans were boiled. Seal the jars while hot.

VEGETABLES 19

CARROTS WITH ORANGE SAUCE

The sweetness of the orange juice will establish the amount of brown sugar needed. If the orange juice is somewhat sour, add a little extra brown sugar. Remember to grate the orange rind before squeezing the juice.

    1 kg carrots
    180 g cooked green peas (1 c)
    30 g cornflour (3 T)
    500 ml fresh, unsweetened
      orange juice (2 c)
    100 g soft brown sugar (½ c)
    75 g seedless raisins (½ c)
    15 ml butter/margarine (1 T)
    5 ml salt (1 t)
    2 ml finely grated orange rind (½ t)

Peel and slice the carrots. Cover the carrot slices with boiling water. Cook quickly till just done and drain. Add the green peas and keep warm.

Mix the cornflour to a paste with a little of the orange juice. Add to the remaining orange juice together with the brown sugar, raisins, butter/margarine, salt and orange rind. Stir continuously and heat the mixture to boiling point. Boil for a minute or so, but be careful not to burn.

Add the hot orange sauce to the carrot mixture and mix lightly. Spoon into a serving dish and serve hot.

Makes 6–8 servings

SWEET POTATOES WITH ORANGE SAUCE

Peel sweet potatoes and slice them. Add a little boiling water and boil the sweet potatoes slowly until soft and dry.

Make the same orange sauce used for the carrots and lightly mix the sweet potatoes with the sauce. Don't break up the sweet potatoes too much.

BAKED MARANKA IN BATTER

Although this recipe is also most suitable for vegetable marrow (which can taste pretty bland and uninteresting if it is not cooked properly) and pumpkin, I usually use marankas (calabash marrows).

The couple of pips I stick into the ground every spring usually bear so many marankas that I can give them away by the basketful and still have enough left to freeze a few months' supply.

1 large maranka/medium
   vegetable marrow
2 ml salt (½ t)
100 g sugar (½ c)
40 g butter/margarine (3 T)
30 ml milk (2 T)
1 extra large egg
70 g cake flour (½ c)
2 ml baking powder (½ t)
125 ml evaporated milk (½ c)
100 g sugar (½ c)

Peel the maranka/vegetable marrow and cut it into 2 cm-thick slices. Remove the pips and cut the flesh into largish chunks. Boil the chunks in the usual way in a little water till just done.

Preheat the oven to 180 °C. Grease a shallow, ovenproof dish with a volume of approximately 2 litres (8 c).

Drain the cooked chunks. Spoon them into the dish. Sprinkle with half the salt.

Beat the sugar, butter/margarine, milk and egg together until well mixed. Sift the flour, baking powder and the remaining salt together and stir into the egg mixture. Spread the batter over the chunks with a fork. Bake the dish uncovered for about 35 minutes till the batter starts to brown.

Heat the evaporated milk and sugar to boiling point. Pour this mixture over the hot dish and leave for a while to soak in.

Makes 6–8 servings

CURRIED RICE

Curried rice is particularly suitable with meat or fish dishes which do not have a sauce of their own, when ordinary white rice would be too dry and uninteresting as an accompaniment.

It is even more delicious if you stir in a few banana slices, roasted nuts or seedless raisins. The dish freezes well.

    400 g rice (2 c)
    1 large onion
    125 g butter/margarine
    1 chicken stock cube
    25 ml Worcestershire sauce (5 t)
    7 ml Aromat/Fondor (1½ t)
    5 ml salt (1 t)
    5 ml curry powder (1 t)
    2 ml turmeric (½ t)
    pinch of cayenne pepper

Boil the rice in plenty of water until soft but not mushy. Rinse in a colander under cold running water and drain well.

Peel the onion and chop it roughly. Sauté it in the butter/margarine. Crumble the chicken stock cube and add to the sautéed onion. Add the Worcestershire sauce, Aromat/Fondor, salt, curry powder, turmeric and cayenne pepper and mix.

Stir the rice gently into the onion mixture. Heat well.

Makes 10–12 servings

THE ORIGINS OF WORCESTERSHIRE SAUCE

During the reign of Queen Victoria, the firm of Lea & Perrins in Worcester, England, was commissioned to make an Indian sauce of vinegar and spices for one of its clients. For one reason or another the barrel of sauce stood forgotten in a cellar for a couple of years, until it was time to clean out the cellar. The sauce was duly tasted after all that time – and Worcestershire sauce was born.

SPINACH FRITTERS

'You know, just as delicious as silage is to cattle, so are these fritters to me,' my husband told me out of the blue one afternoon at table, while helping himself to seconds of these spinach fritters. After he explained to me how silage contains molasses and who knows what else, I realized that, to cows, it is like pudding.

> 500 g shredded spinach (8 c)
> 2 large potatoes
> 2 medium onions
> 140 g self-raising flour (1 c)
> 7 ml salt (1½ t)
> 5 ml dried thyme (1 t)
> pinch of pepper
> 2 extra large eggs
> sunflower oil

Rinse the spinach under cold running water and drain. Stir the wet shreds of spinach in a large saucepan over moderate heat until just done.

Peel the potatoes and onions and grate coarsely. Mix with the spinach, self-raising flour, salt, thyme and pepper. Beat the eggs and stir into the spinach mixture.

Spoon tablespoons of the mixture into shallow, moderately hot sunflower oil in a heavy-based pan. Fry the fritters first on one side till they begin to brown, and then on the other side. Do not fry these fritters at too high a temperature, because this will spoil the taste and appearance. (If the fritters are fried too fast, they turn black and taste bitter.)

Drain the cooked fritters on a paper towel. Serve them hot.

These fritters freeze well.

Makes 20 fritters

BAKED CABBAGE

If you like cabbage, this dish will be as good as pudding.

2 medium onions
75 g butter/margarine (6 T)
375 g shredded cabbage (5 c)
5 ml barbecue spice (1 t)
500 ml milk (2 c)
50 g cake flour (5½ T)
2 eggs
2 ml salt (½ t)
pinch of ground nutmeg
a little grated Cheddar cheese

Preheat the oven to 180 °C. Grease a shallow, ovenproof dish with a volume of about 1,5 litres (6 c).

Peel the onions and chop roughly. Sauté the onions lightly in 30 ml (2 T) of the butter/margarine. Add the cabbage and stir-fry over moderate heat till the cabbage begins to soften. Season with barbecue spice. Set aside.

Heat the milk until it almost reaches boiling point. Melt the remaining 50 g (4 T) butter/margarine and add the flour. Stir the flour mixture for a few minutes over moderate heat till well blended. Add the hot milk gradually and, using a wire whisk, stir till the sauce boils.

Beat the eggs lightly. Stir a little of the hot sauce into the eggs and then whisk the egg mixture into the remaining white sauce. Season with the salt and nutmeg.

Combine the cabbage mixture with the sauce. Spoon this mixture into the dish and sprinkle with the grated cheese. Bake the dish uncovered for about 40 minutes until it starts to brown. Serve hot.

Makes 6 servings

CAULIFLOWER IN BLANKETS

There are two important considerations when making these cauliflower puffs. Firstly, the cauliflower florets must not be wet when they are dipped into the batter, or the batter will not cling to them. Secondly, the puffs must not fry too quickly, because although they may look golden brown and cooked on the outside, on cutting them you may find runny, raw batter between the florets.

If, however, you keep these two considerations in mind when making this dish, it will taste wonderful.

1 medium cauliflower
100 g cake flour (¾ c)
5 ml baking powder (1 t)
5 ml salt (1 t)
2 ml ground nutmeg (½ t)
200 ml milk (¾ c)
1 egg
15 ml butter/margarine (1 T)
sunflower oil

Break the cauliflower into smallish florets. Boil in the usual way in plenty of salted water till just done, but not mushy. Drain the cauliflower very well.

Sift the cake flour, baking powder, salt and nutmeg together. Beat the milk and egg together and mix the milk mixture with the flour mixture. Melt the butter/margarine and stir into the batter.

Fill a medium-sized saucepan halfway with sunflower oil and heat till moderately hot. Fry just a few pieces of cauliflower at a time. Dip the florets in the batter, letting the excess drip off, then fry in the oil till golden brown on both sides.

Drain the cooked pieces of cauliflower on a paper towel. Serve hot.

Makes 6–8 servings

VEGETABLES 25

VEGETABLE PIE WITH BATTER CRUST

This pie has long been one of my favourite main courses on meatless days. Once you have made the pie, you'll discover how easily you can vary the filling with vegetables that are plentiful or on hand.

FILLING
2 medium potatoes
2 medium carrots
2 medium onions
200 g sliced green beans (2 c)
50 g butter/margarine (4 T)
500 ml chicken stock (2 c)
30 g mushroom soup powder (3 T)

CRUST
125 ml milk (½ c)
125 ml sunflower oil (½ c)
1 egg
100 g cake flour (¾ c)
10 ml baking powder (2 t)
pinch of salt

Peel the potatoes, carrots and onions. Dice the potatoes, cut the carrots into julienne strips and slice the onions in rings. Add the green beans and stir-fry the vegetables in the butter/margarine for a few minutes. Add the chicken stock and mushroom soup powder and simmer until the vegetables are just done.

Preheat the oven to 200 °C. Grease a pie dish with a volume of 1,5 litres (6 c). Spoon the filling into the dish.

Beat the milk, sunflower oil and egg together. Sift the cake flour, the baking powder and the salt together. Add the milk mixture and stir to make a smooth batter. Pour the batter over the filling.

Bake the pie uncovered for about 20 minutes until the crust begins to brown. Serve hot.

Makes 6 servings

QUICK GREEN PEA PIE

This pie can also be made with a 410 g tin of canned green peas.

You may also use this crust for an old-fashioned peach pie. Stew dried peaches in weak rooibos tea until tender. See that they are fairly syrupy. Pour the batter on top and bake the pie until golden brown.

FILLING
300 g fresh or frozen green
  peas (1½ c)
30 ml sugar (2 T)
30 ml custard powder (2 T)
2 ml ground ginger (½ t)

CRUST
50 g cake flour (5½ T)
30 ml sugar (2 T)
7 ml baking powder (1½ t)
pinch of salt
30 ml butter/margarine (2 T)
60 ml milk (¼ c)
1 egg

Boil the green peas in the usual way until just tender. Drain and supplement the cooking liquid with water to 250 ml (1 c) if it is less. Preheat the oven to 200 °C.

Mix the sugar, the custard powder and the ginger with a little of the cooking water. Add to the peas and the remaining cooking water. Bring the mixture to the boil. Boil just until the sauce thickens. Spoon the filling into a shallow, ovenproof dish with a volume of 1 litre (4 c).

Sift the cake flour, the sugar, the baking powder and the salt together. Rub in the butter/margarine. Beat the milk and egg together. Beat this mixture into the flour mixture. Pour the batter over the filling.

Bake the pie for 15–20 minutes until the crust is golden brown. Serve hot.

Makes 6 servings

SALAD

In summer, it's pleasant to eat cool, crisp salads that you can rustle up in a moment, while in winter you can tuck into filling, hot salads. And on days when the meal looks a bit skimpy, that jar of beetroot, bean salad (sousboontjies) or curried carrots that you can just take from the fridge will solve the problem beautifully. Salad not only provides an elegant finish to an ordinary plate of food, but also makes it more interesting.

CURRIED CARROTS

I always keep curried carrots on the shelf. When I have to provide a meal in a hurry, without any warning, it's easy to heat a meat pie, make one or two salads and open a jar of curried carrots.

    2 kg carrots
    1 kg onions
    1 litre white vinegar (4 c)
    800 g sugar (4 c)
    150 g seedless raisins (1 c)
    15 ml salt (1 T)
    5 ml whole cloves (1 t)
    5 ml black peppercorns (1 t)
    50 ml cornflour (3 T)
    50 ml curry powder (3 T)

Peel the carrots and slice thinly. Cover the slices with water and boil till just soft.
    Peel and halve the onions. Slice thinly. Cover the onions with boiling water and leave to stand for 15 minutes.
    Drain the carrots and onions. Add the white vinegar, sugar, raisins, salt, cloves and black peppercorns to the vegetables and bring to the boil.
    Mix the cornflour and curry powder with 250 ml (1 c) water. Add the curry mixture to the carrot mixture and boil for about 10 minutes. Stir occasionally.
    Spoon the hot curried carrots into clean, hot jars and seal immediately.

Makes 3,5 litres (14 c) curried carrots

CURRIED CABBAGE

It's inexpensive, easy and delicious to boot!

    1 medium cabbage
    2 medium onions
    300 g sugar (1½ c)
    15 ml cornflour (1 T)
    7 ml medium curry powder (1½ t)
    7 ml mustard powder (1½ t)
    5 ml salt (1 t)
    300 ml white vinegar (1¼ c)

Shred the cabbage finely. Peel the onions and chop coarsely. Boil the cabbage and onions in the usual way, until tender. Drain the vegetables well.
    Mix the sugar, cornflour, curry and mustard powder and salt. Mix with a little of the vinegar. Add the remaining vinegar and boil the sauce for about 5 minutes.
    Add the cabbage mixture and let it simmer well. Spoon into sterilized jars while still hot and seal immediately.

Makes 1,5 litres (6 c) curried cabbage

SALAD 29

HOT RICE SALAD

I agree with Elsabé Burger, my dear neighbour at Yzerfontein, when she says: 'This salad isn't cheap, but one has to splurge occasionally.'

Fortunately, this recipe makes a large quantity and, since it freezes well, there should be enough for more than one meal.

Fresh brown or white mushrooms taste best in this salad, but tinned mushrooms may also be used.

   400 g rice (2 c)
   875 ml boiling water (3½ c)
   2 chicken stock cubes
   3 onions
   1 clove garlic
   1 medium green pepper
   30 ml sunflower oil (2 T)
   250 g mushrooms
   250 g bacon
   1 large tomato
   5 ml salt (1 t)
   pinch of black pepper

Cook the rice in the boiling water to which the chicken stock cubes have been added, until it is soft but not mushy.

Peel the onions and garlic and chop roughly. Halve and seed the green pepper and cut into strips. Braise these vegetables in the sunflower oil until soft.

Wipe the mushrooms with a damp cloth. Cut up the mushrooms and bacon. Peel the tomato and chop roughly. Add the mushrooms, bacon and tomato to the onion mixture and braise till just done. Season with the salt and black pepper.

Mix the vegetable mixture and the rice lightly together with a large fork. Serve the rice salad hot.

Makes about 16 servings

PEARL WHEAT SALAD

The tin of peaches used in this recipe can be replaced with a tin of pineapple pieces of the same size if preferred. For an even more pleasing texture, sprinkle a handful of roasted sunflower seeds on top of the salad just before serving.

200 g pearl wheat (1 c)
1 tin (410 g) peach slices
1 medium onion
1 ripe tomato
½ green pepper
150 g seedless raisins (1 c)
125 ml mayonnaise (½ c)
5 ml salt (1 t)
2 ml medium curry powder (½ t)

Boil the pearl wheat in plenty of water till soft. Drain well and cool.

Drain the peach slices. Peel the onion. Cut up the peach slices, onion, tomato and green pepper. Add the pearl wheat and raisins to the vegetable mixture.

Mix the mayonnaise, the salt and the curry powder. Stir the mayonnaise mixture lightly into the wheat mixture. Chill the salad well before serving.

Makes 6–8 servings

COOKING PEARL WHEAT

Pearl wheat can be most successfully cooked as follows:

Cover the pearl wheat with plenty of water, heat to boiling point and leave to soak overnight. Heat to boiling point again the next day and then drain well.

Or place 200 g (1 c) pearl wheat in a deep microwave dish with a volume of 2 litres (8 c) and add 250 ml (1 c) water. Microwave uncovered on 100% power for about 10 minutes. Stir the pearl wheat, cover the dish and microwave on 100% power for 14 minutes. Leave to stand for approximately 20 minutes.

SALAD 31

HOT POTATO SALAD

Potato salad made this way is often found in Mediterranean countries. The only difference is that the Mediterraneans prefer to use olive oil instead of the sunflower oil that we use.

This salad tastes especially good with T-bone steaks, sausages or fish portions fried in batter.

- 1 kg potatoes
- 2 fat cloves garlic
- 500 g ripe tomatoes
- 1 large onion
- 60 ml sunflower oil (¼ c)
- 7 ml salt (1½ t)
- 5 ml dried basil (1 t)
- 2 ml coarse black pepper (½ t)

Peel the potatoes and the cloves of garlic. Cut the potatoes into fairly large chunks and crush the garlic. Cover the potatoes and garlic with water and boil until the potatoes are done but not mushy.

Peel the tomatoes and onion and chop roughly. Drain the potato chunks. Add the tomatoes, onion, sunflower oil, salt, basil and black pepper to the potatoes. Mix everything lightly with a large fork.

Serve the salad hot.

Makes 6 servings

IN THE MICROWAVE OVEN

Peel and cut the potatoes and garlic according to the recipe. Then place the potato chunks and the garlic in a deep microwave dish. Add 60 ml (¼ c) water. Cover the dish and microwave the contents on 100% power for approximately 10 minutes until soft but not mushy. Drain the potatoes and finish making the salad according to the recipe.

MIXED BEETROOT SALAD WITH MAYONNAISE

When you cook beetroot, you must guard against 'bleeding' by leaving the skin and the roots of the beetroot intact. When you want to remove the leaves, you should twist them off rather than cutting them off. Also, do not pierce the beetroot with a skewer to test if it is cooked and tender. If the skin rubs off easily, it is done.

Young, fresh beetroot leaves are delicious when used uncooked in salads. They may also be cooked like spinach for a vegetable dish with a difference.

4 largish beetroot
1 large potato
1 large onion
1 medium green pepper
200 ml mayonnaise (¾ c)
60 ml brown vinegar (¼ c)
15 ml sugar (1 T)
1 ml salt (¼ t)
pinch of pepper

Twist off the leaves of each beetroot about 3 cm from the bulb. Wash the beetroot well. Boil in their skins in a pot of water till done. Drain and cover the beetroot with cold water.

Boil the potato in its jacket until tender. Drain and cover with cold water.

Skin and dice the beetroot and potato. Peel the onion and chop roughly. Halve and seed the green pepper and then cut it into short strips.

Mix the mayonnaise, brown vinegar, sugar, salt and pepper until well blended. Add the diced beetroot and potato, the chopped onion and the strips of green pepper and mix lightly.

Chill the salad before serving. Store in a closed container in the refrigerator.

Makes about 15 servings

MOTHER-IN-LAW'S BEAN SALAD (SOUSBOONTJIES)

No-one can make bean salad like my mother-in-law. You may be surprised to see how much sugar she uses, but she comes from a generation which measured butter and sugar with a liberal hand. I have on occasion used less sugar, but then the bean salad just doesn't taste as good as my mother-in-law's.

500 g sugar beans (2½ c)
400 g sugar (2 c)
125 ml brown vinegar (½ c)
2 ml salt (½ t)

Spread the sugar beans out on a table and remove all impurities. Cover the beans with plenty of water and soak them overnight. (Or bring the beans to the boil in plenty of water and cook them for approximately 10 minutes. Remove the saucepan from the heat and leave the beans to soak for about 2 hours.)

Drain the soaked beans. Cover with fresh boiling water and cook till well done. They should have a floury texture when rubbed between the fingers. (Add a knob of butter/margarine if the water threatens to froth over the edge of the saucepan.) Remove the lid of the saucepan towards the end so that the beans can cook fairly dry.

Add the sugar, brown vinegar and salt, and simmer slowly until the sauce has the required thickness. Leave to cool.

Makes 14 servings

TIPS FOR SOUSBOONTJIES

Always store the dried beans in an airtight container in the freezer. This prevents infestation by mites.

Always add sugar and salt only after the beans are soft.

The secret of marvellous sousboontjies is apparently to stir in a tablespoon of golden syrup towards the end.

NOODLE SALAD

When you have to cater for a crowd of people, noodle salad is a good stand-by. I prepare it without the mayonnaise and store it in a jar in the refrigerator. When we want to use the salad, I take out just enough salad and stir in mayonnaise.

   250 g screw noodles (3 c)
   1 large tomato
   1 large onion
   1 medium green pepper
   30 ml sunflower oil (2 T)
   30 ml white vinegar (2 T)
   30 ml chutney (2 T)
   30 ml tomato sauce (2 T)
   30 ml sugar (2 T)
   7 ml medium curry powder (1½ t)
   5 ml salt (1 t)
   125 ml mayonnaise (½ c)

Boil the noodles in plenty of water until just done. Drain the noodles and cover them with cold water.

Peel the tomato and onion and chop roughly. Halve and seed the green pepper and cut it into shortish strips. Braise the tomato, onion and green pepper in the sunflower oil till tender.

Mix the vinegar, chutney, tomato sauce, sugar, curry powder and salt together. Stir the curry mixture into the vegetable mixture and simmer for a while.

Drain the noodles very well. Add the vegetable sauce and mix lightly. Stir in the mayonnaise just before serving.

Serve the salad hot or cold.

Makes 14 servings

VARIATION

Peel one or two carrots and grate them coarsely. Braise together with the tomato, onion and green pepper in slightly more oil than the amount indicated in the recipe. Then finish making the salad according to the recipe.

FRIDGE CABBAGE SALAD

This wonderful salad may be kept in its sauce in the fridge for a month. When you want to use it, spoon out the amount required and drain just before serving.

    1 largish cabbage
    1 medium green pepper
    1 medium onion
    200 g sugar (1 c)
    125 ml white vinegar (½ c)
    5 ml mustard powder (1 t)
    5 ml aniseed or celery seed (1 t)
    2 ml salt (½ t)
    200 ml sunflower oil (¾ c)

Finely shred the cabbage. Halve and seed the green pepper and cut into thin strips. Peel the onion and slice into thin rings. Mix the cabbage, the green pepper and the onion. Sprinkle with half the sugar.

Boil the remaining sugar, vinegar, mustard powder, aniseed or celery seed and salt. Add the sunflower oil and bring to the boil again. Pour the boiling sauce over the cabbage mixture. Cool and store in an airtight container in the refrigerator.

Makes 12–14 servings

COLESLAW DRESSING

Moisten cabbage shreds with some of this excellent fridge dressing for a tasty salad prepared in a jiffy.

    1 tin (440 g) crushed pineapple
    1 tin (397 g) condensed milk
    250 ml mayonnaise (1 c)
    100 g coarsely grated Cheddar cheese (1 c)

Mix the pineapple, condensed milk, mayonnaise and Cheddar cheese. Store in a closed container in the refrigerator.

Makes 1 litre (4 c) salad dressing

SWEET AND SOUR CUCUMBERS

I am quite besotted with these cucumbers. Our family eats slices of them just as they are with fish dishes or with cold meat. Alternatively I cut them up into mixed salads. You could also add slices of these cucumbers to cheese or meat sandwiches to make them taste even better.

I find fresh, young English cucumbers most suitable for this recipe.

> 500 ml white vinegar (2 c)
> 5 ml mustard seed (1 t)
> 5 ml allspice berries (1 t)
> 10 cloves
> stick of cinnamon
> 1 bay leaf
> 1 kg cucumbers
> 140 g salt (½ c)
> iced water and ice cubes
> 50 g sugar (4 T)
> dill seed
> black peppercorns

Bring the white vinegar, mustard seed, allspice berries, cloves, cinnamon and bay leaf to the boil in an enamel or stainless steel saucepan. Remove from the stove and set aside to infuse.

Cut the cucumbers into 5 mm-thick slices. Layer the slices in an enamel or stainless steel dish and sprinkle salt over every layer. Cover the slices with iced water and ice cubes. Leave for 4 hours.

Drain the cucumber slices. Rinse in a colander under cold running water. Place in a large enamel or stainless steel saucepan. Pour the flavoured vinegar through a sieve and add to the cucumber slices with the sugar. Slowly bring it to the boil. Cook for only 5 minutes.

Place a few dill seeds and one or two peppercorns in each clean, hot jar. Pack the cucumber slices in them and fill each jar to overflowing with the spiced vinegar in which the slices of cucumber were cooked. Seal the jars immediately.

Makes 1,5 litres (6 c) cucumber slices

SALAD

FISH

Fish and chips, popular all over the world, is not the only delicious and economical fish dish that exists. Ordinary fish cakes, made from a tin of pilchards, can be a gourmet treat if properly made. And there won't be a crumb of snoek tart or tuna pie left over – if you have the right recipes. If you're having guests to a meal, you can show off with litchi fish. Or what about fish with avocado cream?

FISH WITH PINEAPPLE SAUCE

This fried fish is light in colour but is covered with a nice crisp crust because it is rolled in a mixture of flour and cornflour. Place the fish portions in a row on a large serving platter and spoon sweet-and-sour pineapple sauce on each portion. With rice and a salad, this is a simple, tasty meal.

I also use haddock for this recipe. The colour of the haddock makes the cooked fish look most appetizing.

FISH FILLETS
800 g frozen hake fillets
lemon juice
salt and pepper
1 extra large egg
40 g cake flour (4 T)
40 g cornflour (4 T)
sunflower oil

PINEAPPLE SAUCE
1 green pepper
60 g chopped spring onions (½ c)
15 ml butter/margarine (1 T)
1 tin (440 g) pineapple pieces
15 ml white vinegar (1 T)
15 ml cornflour (1 T)
10 ml soya sauce (2 t)
pinch of salt

Remove the skin from the fish fillets. Halve the fillets and leave them to thaw. Sprinkle with a little lemon juice and season with salt and pepper. Beat the egg. Mix the cake flour and cornflour.

Dip the pieces of fish one at a time into the beaten egg and then roll them in the flour mixture until they are completely coated. Fry the pieces of fish on both sides in moderately hot, shallow sunflower oil till done. Keep hot.

Halve and seed the green pepper. Cut into strips. Sauté the green pepper and spring onions in the butter/margarine. Drain the pineapple pieces and reserve 125 ml (½ c) of the pineapple juice. Add the drained pineapple pieces to the green pepper mixture. Mix the pineapple juice with the white vinegar, cornflour, soya sauce and salt. Stir this mixture into the green pepper mixture and boil until the sauce is thick and clear.

Serve the pineapple sauce with the fish.

Makes 6–8 servings

FISH 39

LITCHI FISH

This dish was very popular at Boland dinner parties a couple of years ago. I make it from ordinary hake fillets because I always keep some in the freezer, but if you want to show off a bit, you can use kingklip fillets and garnish the dish with fried mushroom slices and fresh dill instead of parsley.

When I make this dish in a hurry for my family, I use the fish fillets with skin and all, but for guests I pull off the skin while the fillets are still frozen.

You will enjoy this dish more if you use litchis without stones. But because stoned litchis are much more expensive than those with stones, I buy the latter kind and stone them myself.

> 800 g frozen fish fillets
> 1 tin (410 g) whole litchis
> 125 ml water (½ c)
> 1 packet mushroom soup powder
> fresh parsley

Preheat the oven to 180 °C. Grease a shallow, ovenproof dish with a volume of about 2,5 litres (10 c).

Cut the fish fillets into portions and place them in the dish. Drain the litchis and retain the fluid. Mix the litchi fluid, the water and mushroom soup powder thoroughly. Pour this mixture over the fish. Cover the dish.

Bake the dish for about 45 minutes until the fish is cooked. Baste occasionally with the sauce that gathers among the pieces of fish in the dish.

Remove the cover and arrange the litchis over the fish. Bake the dish for a few minutes until the litchis are hot and the sauce is thick.

Garnish the dish with parsley and serve the fish piping hot.

Makes 6 servings

FISH WITH AVOCADO CREAM

This easy-to-make fish dish is suitable even for a dinner party, because it not only tastes delicious, but looks good too. Served with salads it is an excellent main course.

FISH FILLETS
800 g frozen hake fillets
juice of 1 lemon
5 ml salt (1 t)
pinch each of coarse black pepper, cayenne pepper, cinnamon and ground nutmeg
15 ml butter/margarine (1 T)
15 ml sesame seeds (1 T)

AVOCADO CREAM
1 smallish ripe avacado
30 ml lemon juice (2 T)
30 ml cream (2 T)
5 ml prepared mustard (1 t)
few drops Tabasco sauce
salt and pepper

Preheat the oven to 180 °C.

Remove the skin from the hake fillets. Arrange the fillets next to each other, top and tail alternating, in a shallow, oven-proof dish. Sprinkle the fish with lemon juice and season with salt and spices. Dot with the butter/margarine. Cover the dish. Bake the fish fillets for about 40 minutes. Remove the cover and sprinkle the fish with sesame seed. Grill the fish for a few minutes until it starts browning.

Peel the avocado, remove the pip and purée the flesh. Beat together the lemon juice, cream, mustard and Tabasco sauce till well blended. Add the avocado purée to the cream mixture and combine well. Season to taste with salt and pepper.

Serve the cold avocado cream with the hot fish fillets.

Makes 6–8 servings

HAKE BAKE

I use the fish fillets with skin and all unless I'm making the dish for guests. It's quite easy to pull the skin off while the fillets are still frozen.

It is preferable not to use floury potatoes in this dish, because the potato slices will disintegrate too easily.

    3 medium potatoes
    2 cloves garlic
    250 ml chicken stock (1 c)
    400–600 g frozen hake fillets
    salt and pepper
    2 ripe, medium tomatoes
    1 large onion
    50 g butter/margarine (4 T)
    60 g fresh breadcrumbs (1 c)

Peel the potatoes and cut into thickish slices. Peel and crush the garlic cloves and add to the potato slices in a saucepan. Add the chicken stock and cook the potato slices till nearly tender.

Place the hake fillets in a shallow, oven-proof dish with a volume of about 2 litres (8 c). Season the fish lightly with salt and pepper. Arrange the potato slices on top of the fish and add the stock in which they were cooked.

Peel the tomatoes and onion and chop them roughly. Braise in half of the butter/margarine till just done. Spoon the tomato mixture over the potato slices and season lightly with salt and pepper. Melt the remaining butter/margarine and mix lightly with the breadcrumbs. Scatter the crumbs over the dish.

Cover the dish. Bake the dish for about half an hour at 180 °C. Uncover and bake for another half an hour.

Serve the dish hot.

Makes 4–6 servings

HADDOCK PARCELS

This recipe can also be made with hake fillets. If you have fresh mushrooms, slice a handful and use instead of the canned mushrooms. The bacon may be omitted if preferred.

I always serve the fish fillets in their foil wrappers since in this way none of the sauce is lost. Unfold the foil and trim it slightly smaller to neaten the edges. Garnish the fish fillets with a sprig of parsley or fennel just before serving.

   800 g frozen haddock fillets
   125 g bacon
   1 medium onion
   30 ml butter/margarine (2 T)
   1 tin (285 g) sliced mushrooms
   30 g mushroom soup powder (3 T)
   lemon juice

Thaw the haddock fillets. Cut a rectangle of 30 cm x 20 cm from aluminium foil for each fillet. (If the fillets are small, place them next to each other, two at a time, head to tail, to constitute one serving.) Preheat the oven to 200 °C.

Cut the rind from the bacon and chop up the bacon. Peel the onion and chop it roughly. Sauté the bacon and onion in the butter/margarine. Drain the mushrooms and fry lightly together with the bacon mixture. Sprinkle the soup powder over the mixture and stir.

Place the fish fillets on the aluminium foil and sprinkle a little lemon juice on each fillet. Spoon the bacon mixture on top of the fish. Fold the foil tightly around the fish to seal.

Place the fish parcels on a baking sheet. Bake for approximately 25 minutes till done. Serve the fish hot.

Makes 4–6 servings

44 FISH

TUNA PIE

This pie surely has the quickest possible crust, because with a little rub here and a sprinkle there, the crust is on the pie. Tuna pie served with thick slices of tomato, lettuce and curried carrots makes a pleasant light supper.

FILLING
2 medium onions
50 g butter/margarine (4 T)
50 g cake flour (5½ T)
5 ml mustard powder (1 t)
5 ml salt (1 t)
pinch of pepper
450 ml milk (1¾ c)
2 tins (200 g each) tuna
3 hard-boiled eggs
30 ml finely chopped parsley (2 T)

CRUST
100 g cake flour (¾ c)
1 ml salt (¼ t)
pinch of pepper
50 g butter/margarine (4 T)
70 g finely grated Cheddar cheese (1 c)

Preheat the oven to 200 °C. Grease a shallow, ovenproof dish with a volume of about 1,5 litres (6 c). Peel and chop the onions and sauté in the butter/margarine. Over medium heat, stir the flour, mustard powder, salt and pepper into the onions and gradually add the milk. Stir continuously and bring it to the boil.

Drain and flake the tuna. Finely chop the eggs. Mix the tuna, eggs and parsley lightly with the onion mixture. Spoon the filling into the dish.

Sift the cake flour, salt and pepper. Rub in the butter/margarine. Add the cheese and mix lightly. Place this mixture over the filling. Bake for 20 minutes. Serve hot.

Makes 4–6 servings

SNOEK TART

If I do not have to make this tart for a large number of people, I make two smaller tarts instead of one large one. We eat one tart immediately and I freeze the other one for later use. The smoked snoek can be replaced with cooked haddock.

CRUST
275 g cake flour (2 c)
2 ml salt (½ t)
pinch of cayenne pepper
200 g finely grated Cheddar cheese (3 c)
175 g butter/margarine (¾ c)

FILLING
500 g smoked snoek
5 eggs
375 ml milk (1½ c)
15 ml Worcestershire sauce (1 T)

Preheat the oven to 180 °C. Grease a pie dish with a volume of 2,5 litres (10 c).

Sift together the flour, salt and cayenne pepper. Add the Cheddar cheese and the butter/margarine and mix well to form a soft dough. Press the dough fairly thinly into the pie dish. Roll out the remaining dough to a thickness of about 1 cm on a sheet of waxed paper. Cut into strips. Chill the uncooked crust and the strips.

Flake the snoek and remove all bones. Hard-boil three of the eggs, shell them and grate coarsely. Beat the remaining two eggs, milk and Worcestershire sauce together. Mix the snoek, grated eggs and milk mixture together lightly.

Spoon the filling into the crust. Arrange the dough strips on top.

Bake the pie for about 45 minutes till cooked and set. Serve lukewarm.

Makes 10–12 servings

PILCHARD BOBOTIE

We usually eat fluffy white rice, banana salad, stewed peaches and chutney with pilchard bobotie.

The recipe may successfully be doubled to make 8–10 servings, in which case the bobotie should be baked for a little longer.

- 1 slice white bread, 2,5 cm thick
- 300 ml milk (1¼ c)
- 1 large onion
- 50 g butter/margarine (4 T)
- 5 ml medium curry powder (1 t)
- 1 tin (425 g) pilchards in tomato sauce
- 30 ml seedless raisins (2 T)
- 30 ml lemon juice (2 T)
- 2 eggs
- 2 ml salt (½ t)
- 2 lemon leaves

Preheat the oven to 190 °C. Grease a shallow, ovenproof dish with a volume of approximately 1 litre (4 c).

Finely trim the crusts from the white bread. Soak the bread in the milk. Press most of the milk from the bread (reserve the milk) and crumble the bread.

Peel the onion and chop finely. Sauté the onion in the butter/margarine. Add the curry powder and fry lightly.

Drain and flake the pilchards. Mix lightly with the bread, onion, raisins and lemon juice. Beat together the eggs, the milk in which the bread was soaked, and the salt. Mix half of the egg mixture with the fish mixture and spoon it into the dish. Pour the remaining egg mixture on top. Press the lemon leaves into the fish mixture like funnels.

Bake the bobotie for about 40 minutes until cooked and set. Serve hot.

Makes 4–5 servings

FIBRE-RICH FISH CAKES

Nothing can compare with these fish cakes as regards value for money, because you get a full dozen fish cakes from one single tin of pilchards. I prefer pilchards in natural sauce to those in tomato sauce.

By the way, these fish cakes are also excellent cold in a lunch tin or as a sandwich filling.

1 tin (425 g) pilchards
1 largish onion
1 egg
50 ml bran (3 T)
40 g cake flour (4 T)
2 ml salt (½ t)
pinch of pepper
sunflower oil

Lightly mash the pilchards together with their sauce. Peel the onion and chop it finely. Beat the egg.

Mix all the ingredients except the sunflower oil lightly with a fork.

Heat a little sunflower oil in a heavy-based pan till moderately hot. Spoon dessertspoons of the fish mixture into the hot oil. Fry the fish cakes on both sides until brown. (Be careful of spluttering oil.) Drain the cooked fish cakes on paper towelling and serve.

Makes 12–14 fish cakes

QUICK SAUCE FOR FISH CAKES

Mix together 200 ml (¾ c) unflavoured yoghurt, 60 ml (¼ c) mayonnaise, 30 ml (2 T) each of finely chopped parsley and spring onions and a pinch of dried basil. Season the sauce with a little salt and pepper and chill until cold.

MEAT

Veal ribs over the coals! Good quality veal ribs, properly prepared, are tender and succulent. And don't forget about that secret seasoning sauce for seasoning the meat at a braai. It's extremely satisfying to make your own boerewors – not to mention making your own corned beef. Children and adults alike are crazy about golden brown fried chicken, crisp and tasty, just as the Americans make it.

GARLIC KEBABS

This dish is Portuguese in origin and very flavourful. Years ago I had to write an article on Portuguese food when I came across this recipe in one of my cookbooks. When I want to make a treat for just Chris and me, I prepare this dish for us to savour at sunset in the garden over a mug of beer. We eat it with rice or potatoes and a bowl of mixed green salad.

500 g pork fillet, cut 2,5 cm thick
500 g leg or shoulder of lamb, cut 2,5 cm thick
4 cloves garlic
30 ml sherry (2 T)
15 ml finely chopped mint (1 T)
15 ml paprika (1 T)
15 ml sunflower oil (1 T)
10 ml grated orange rind (2 t)
5 ml dried origanum (1 t)
5 ml sugar (1 t)
1 ml coarse black pepper (¼ t)
5 ml salt (1 t)

Cut the meat into 2,5 cm cubes. Peel and crush the garlic.

Mix all the ingredients except the meat and salt. Add the meat to this mixture and combine well. Cover the dish and marinate for about 2 hours. Stir occasionally.

Thread the cubes of meat onto skewers and season with the salt. Grill the kebabs in the oven over an oven roasting dish lined with aluminium foil until done. Baste the meat occasionally with the garlic mixture or pan drippings and turn the skewers at regular intervals. Serve the kebabs immediately.

Makes 4–6 servings

PIQUANT POTATO DISH

This is a colourful, appetizing substitute for rice to serve with kebabs.

Boil a couple of potatoes in their jackets till tender. Remove the skins and cut the potatoes into fairly thick slices.

Make a good thick tomato and onion sauce, adding a clove of garlic and a little curry powder. Sweeten with a little sugar and season to taste with salt and pepper.

Place alternate layers of potato slices and sauce in a serving dish and heat the dish until steaming.

Sprinkle with a little finely chopped parsley just before serving.

MEAT 49

BARBECUE SEASONING SAUCE

We are never without this sauce. Even on holiday, we always take a bottle with us. If you have used it once, ordinary salt and pepper just aren't good enough. Braai your meat in the usual way until almost done. Sprinkle the sauce over the meat and braai it for a minute or so. Turn the meat over, sprinkle with some more sauce and braai for another couple of minutes.

- 375 ml brown vinegar (1½ c)
- 250 ml water (1 c)
- 200 g salt (¾ c)
- 2 large onions
- 6 fat cloves garlic
- 30 ml Worcestershire sauce (2 T)
- 15 ml tomato sauce (1 T)
- 5 ml paprika (1 t)
- 5 ml white pepper (1 t)
- 10 cloves
- 10 black peppercorns
- 1 ml cayenne pepper (¼ t)

Heat the brown vinegar and water. Add the salt and stir till dissolved.

Peel the onions and garlic and chop finely. Add to the vinegar mixture. Add the remaining ingredients and mix well.

Pour the mixture into a jar and let it mature for 10–12 days. After that, pour it through a sieve into a bottle. Store the sauce in a cool place.

Makes 625 ml (2½ c) seasoning sauce

SAVOURY GRAVY POWDER

Mix the following and use it instead of ordinary gravy powder: 1 packet (500 g) cornflour, 2 packets (250 g each) gravy powder, 2 packets brown onion soup powder, 1 packet cream of tomato soup powder and 1 packet cream of mushroom soup powder.

VEAL RIB OVER THE COALS

When we slaughter a young ox, we cut the ribs into strips, roll them up and freeze them for marinating and braaiing over the coals at a later stage. I was at first very sceptical about this rib-braai suggested by my husband Chris, but quickly changed my opinion. The secret is to use only prime grade veal ribs.

    2 medium onions
    30 ml sunflower oil (2 T)
    15 ml medium curry powder (1 T)
    125 ml brown vinegar (½ c)
    125 ml water (½ c)
    75 g sugar (6 T)
    2 bay leaves
    1,75 kg veal rib, cut across the ribs in a 7 cm-wide strip
    7 ml salt (1½ t)

Peel the onions and cut into rings. Sauté the rings in the sunflower oil. Add the curry powder and fry lightly. Stir in the brown vinegar, water, sugar and bay leaves. Leave to cool. Lay the veal rib in the mixture and marinate it for 24 hours. Turn the meat once or twice.

Add the salt to the marinade and boil the veal rib in it until tender.

Cut the rib into largish pieces. Braai the pieces over moderately hot coals until they start to brown. (If the coals are too hot, the meat can easily become too dark.) Baste the meat at regular intervals with the marinade while braaiing.

Boil the remaining marinade quite briskly in an uncovered saucepan until it forms a thick sauce.

Cut the meat into portions and serve immediately with the sauce.

Makes 6 servings

T-BONES WITH PEPPER SAUCE

Grill T-bones in the usual way over the coals or fry in a ribbed frying pan to your preferred degree of doneness. Season with salt and pepper and serve with one of these tasty pepper sauces.

CREAMED PEPPER SAUCE
1 smallish onion
40 g butter/margarine (3 T)
30 ml canned green peppercorns (2 T)
30 ml brandy (2 T)
5 ml prepared mustard (1 t)
250 ml cream (1 c)
2 ml salt (½ t)
chopped parsley

Peel the onion and chop finely. Sauté in the butter/margarine. Slightly crush the peppercorns and add together with the brandy and mustard to the onion mixture. Boil the mixture briskly without a lid till almost all the liquid has evaporated. Add the cream and salt and cook the sauce over moderate heat till thick. Sprinkle with parsley before serving.

Makes 275 ml (a little more than 1 c) sauce

PEPPER MAYONNAISE
15 ml butter/margarine (1 T)
2 eggs
80 g sugar (6 T)
75 ml white vinegar (5 T)
30 ml canned green peppercorns (2 T)
2 ml salt (½ t)
125 ml mayonnaise (½ c)

Stir the butter/margarine in a heavy-based pan with a fork. Add the eggs and beat with the fork. Add the sugar, the white vinegar, peppercorns and salt.

Cook the sauce over moderate heat till it thickens, stirring continuously. Finally stir in the mayonnaise and serve the sauce with the grilled T-bone steaks.

Makes 325 ml (1⅓ c) sauce

BABY'S BEAN POT

On many occasions, when the miserable weather in Cape Town proved too much for me, I would get into my car on a particularly rainy Saturday and go and visit my aunt Baby Stanford in Bellville. The two of us would have a good old chat and eat big helpings of her wonderful neck of mutton and bean stew.

    500 g speckled sugar beans (2½ c)
    1 kg neck of mutton, sliced
    15 ml salt (1 T)
    1 ml pepper (¼ t)
    60 ml sunflower oil (¼ c)
    3 large onions
    500 ml boiling water (2 c)
    15 ml cake flour (1 T)
    15 ml chutney (1 T)
    15 ml brown vinegar (1 T)
    15 ml sugar (1 T)
    7 ml medium curry powder (1½ t)
    5 ml Worcestershire sauce (1 t)
    5 ml turmeric (1 t)

Spread the beans on a table and remove all impurities. Cover the beans with plenty of water and soak overnight. (Or boil the beans in plenty of water and cook for 10 minutes. Remove the saucepan from the stove and allow to soak for 2 hours.)

Drain the soaked beans. Cover with fresh boiling water and boil till very soft. They should be floury in texture when rubbed between the fingers. (Add a knob of butter/margarine if the water threatens to boil over the edge of the saucepan.) Drain the cooked beans.

Season the meat with the salt and pepper and fry quickly on both sides in the oil till brown. Remove the meat. Peel the onion and chop roughly. Fry in the same oil in which the meat was fried. Return the meat to the pot with the onions. Add the boiling water and cook till tender.

Mix the remaining ingredients, add to the meat and cook through. Add the beans and heat right through.

Makes 6 servings

OX-TONGUE IN TOMATO AND MUSHROOM SAUCE

This is without a doubt the best recipe for ox-tongue in my possession. If the tongue is corned, it must first be desalted for an hour in cold water.

When I have to prepare a meal for a crowd of people, I like to use this recipe because it can easily be stretched. I often substitute cooked beef for the ox-tongue because it is cheaper. A little finely chopped fresh basil is an ideal garnish.

   1 ox-tongue
   2 medium onions
   30 ml sunflower oil (2 T)
   1 tin (285 g) sliced mushrooms
   125 ml tomato sauce (½ c)
   125 ml brown vinegar (½ c)
   30 ml sugar (2 T)
   10 ml prepared mustard (2 t)
   10 ml salt (2 t)
   5 ml dried basil (1 t)
   1 ml pepper (¼ t)

Cover the tongue with water and cook it until it is tender. Leave it to cool in the cooking liquid. Pull off the skin and cut the tongue into thin slices.

Peel the onions and chop roughly. Fry in the sunflower oil until soft. Add the mushrooms and their liquid, the tomato sauce, brown vinegar, sugar, mustard, salt, basil and pepper and cook the sauce for about 8 minutes over moderate heat.

Place a layer of tongue slices in an ovenproof dish with a volume of 2 litres (8 c). Spoon a layer of sauce over the meat. Repeat the layers until everything has been used. End with a layer of sauce.

Bake the dish for 30 minutes at 180 °C.

Makes 6–8 servings

CORNED BEEF

When it is slaughtering time on the farm, the 'pickle barrel' – my big jam pot – is at the ready. Cuts from the ox carcass most suitable for pickling are the shoulder, silverside, brisket, topside and tongue. We never make the cuts thicker than 10 cm.

When cooking the corned beef, add a couple of peeled carrots and one or two onions studded with cloves to add flavour.

BRINE
750 g coarse salt (3½ c)
100 g soft brown sugar (½ c)
60g saltpetre (3 T)
30 g bicarbonate of soda (2 T)
5 litres boiling water (20 c)
3 cloves garlic (optional)
12 bay leaves
5 ml black peppercorns (1 t)
5 ml allspice berries (1 t)

MEAT
5–10 kg beef

Dissolve the salt, brown sugar, saltpetre and bicarbonate of soda in the boiling water. Pour the solution through a muslin cloth into a large plastic dish or stainless steel container.

Crush the garlic. Tie it, together with the bay leaves, peppercorns and allspice berries, in a piece of muslin and add to the hot brine. Leave to cool.

Place the cuts of meat in the brine with a non-metallic weight on top. Leave in the brine for about 5 days, depending on the thickness of the joints. Pieces cut thinner than 7,5 cm should stay in the brine for about 3 days. Keep in the refrigerator or cool-room. Turn the joints every day.

Rinse the corned meat. (Desalt it for an hour in cold water if it has been in the brine for quite a long time.) Cover with fresh water and slowly bring to the boil. Cook the meat slowly over moderate heat until done. Let it cool in the liquid in which it was cooked.

FILLED MEAT ROLL

This is baked in a loaf tin and looks like a meatloaf – until you discover the filling. The filling can be varied by adding finely chopped cooked ham or roughly grated Vienna sausages and gherkins.

500 g minced beef
500 g pork sausage meat
1 medium carrot
1 medium onion
30 ml sunflower oil (2 T)
4 eggs
2 slices white bread
30 ml finely chopped parsley (2 T)
7 ml salt (1½ t)
1 ml pepper (¼ t)
75 g coarsely grated Cheddar cheese (¾ c)

Mix the minced beef and pork lightly. Peel the carrot and the onion and grate coarsely. Lightly sauté the carrot and onion in the sunflower oil.

Beat two of the eggs and hard-boil the remaining two. Crumble both the slices of white bread.

Combine the meat with the vegetable mixture, the beaten eggs, breadcrumbs, parsley, salt and pepper. Roll the meat mixture on a piece of aluminium foil to form a rectangle of about 40 cm x 30 cm.

Grate the boiled eggs roughly over the meat. Sprinkle with cheese. Roll up the meat with its filling like a Swiss roll. Place the roll in a loaf tin with a volume of 1,5 litres (6 c). Cover the tin.

Bake the meat roll for about 1½ hours at 180 °C till done. Remove the covering, then set the oven to 220 °C and bake a little longer till nicely browned on top. Baste occasionally with the sauce that collects in the tin.

Serve hot or cold.

Makes 8 servings

TOMATO FRIKKADELS

My main requirement for frikkadels is that they should be like my mother's – quite light and juicy in texture and not at all hard and compacted.

Serve rice with these frikkadels so that none of the exceptional sauce is wasted.

Other flavours of soup powder, such as oxtail or mushroom, may be used instead of tomato soup powder.

    4 medium tomatoes
    2 large onions
    30 ml sunflower oil (2 T)
    1 kg minced beef
    50 g oats (½ c)
    125 ml milk (½ c)
    30 ml brown vinegar (2 T)
    15 ml Worcestershire sauce (1 T)
    10 ml salt (2 t)
    1 ml pepper (¼ t)
    125 ml water (½ c)
    30 ml cream of tomato soup
      powder (2 T)

Preheat the oven to 180 °C.

Peel the tomatoes and onions and chop roughly. Braise in the sunflower oil till soft. Mix half of the tomato and onion mixture lightly with the minced beef and the oats. Add the milk, brown vinegar, Worcestershire sauce, salt and pepper and mix together well.

Shape large frikkadels from the mixture and place them quite close together in a shallow, ovenproof dish with a volume of about 2,5 litres (10 c).

Mix the water and soup powder and pour it over the frikkadels. Cover the dish.

Bake the frikkadels for an hour. Spoon the remaining tomato and onion mixture over the frikkadels. Continue baking without a cover until nicely browned on top.

Makes 14 large frikkadels

58 MEAT

BOEREWORS

This recipe will win hands down if you are looking for the best boerewors in the Waterberg. The people of Nylstroom will point out a new church, the building of which was made possible thanks to this recipe and an energetic church council.

    150 g whole coriander (2 c)
    125 g allspice berries (1¼ c)
    32 kg beef
    10 kg pork
    8 kg pork speck
    425 g salt (1½ c)
    100 g coarsely ground black pepper (½ c)
    70 g ground cloves (½ c)
    50 ml ground nutmeg (3 T)
    40 ml white pepper (2½ T)
    1,5 kg oats (15 c)
    1,25 litres brown vinegar (5 c)
    about 1 kg pork casings

Heat a layer of whole coriander in a heavy-based pot and keep stirring until it is roasted to a light brown. Repeat with the remaining coriander. Crush the coriander and the allspice berries by rolling with a bottle or pounding in a mortar. Sift to get rid of the husks.

Cut the beef and pork into pieces about 5 cm x 5 cm and the speck into smaller cubes. Spread it all out on a table.

Mix the coriander, allspice, salt, black pepper, cloves, nutmeg and white pepper. Sprinkle this mixture over the meat and mix by hand. Mince and spread out on the table again. Scatter the oats over the meat and sprinkle the brown vinegar on top. Mix lightly with the fingers using a lifting motion – do not knead.

Rinse the casings in water. Fill lightly with the sausage meat – they should be just well filled without any pockets of air.

Makes 50 kg boerewors

BOEREWORS PIES

Forty years ago, my mother-in-law's pies used to be sold at a café in Windhoek. Every morning before school my husband (then a young lad) had to deliver the basket of pies, carefully covered in a white cloth, to the café.

    1 kg boerewors meat
    200 ml water (¾ c)
    30 g oxtail soup powder (3 T)
    800 g cake flour (6 c)
    30 ml baking powder (2 T)
    5 ml salt (1 t)
    450 g ice cold butter/margarine (2 c)
    3 extra large eggs
    60 ml white vinegar (¼ c)
    sunflower oil

Mix the boerewors meat with 125 ml (½ c) of the water and cook till done and full of gravy. Add the soup powder and cook until the gravy is thick. Spoon the meat into an oven pan and leave to cool. Divide into 36 equal portions when cold.

Sift together the cake flour, the baking powder and the salt. Coarsely grate the butter/margarine on top and then rub it into the flour mixture.

Beat together the eggs, remaining water and white vinegar. Add a little at a time to the flour mixture to make a dough. Cover the dough and let it rest for a while.

Roll some of the dough out thinly on a floured pastry board. Cut out circles about 13 cm in diameter. Moisten the edge of each pastry circle with cold water. Spoon a portion of filling onto the middle of each circle and fold the dough over to make a half-moon shape. Press the edges together well and crimp them.

Fry the pies quickly in hot, deep sunflower oil till golden brown. Drain the cooked pies on paper towelling.

Makes 3 dozen pies

BOBOTIE

Years ago, when I worked on the TV Home Kitchen programme, Swapolina, a member of the recording team, brought me her mother-in-law's bobotie recipe. It's a very easy recipe and the bobotie looks as it tastes – mouthwatering.

The lemon leaves can be replaced with fresh bay leaves or even young orange leaves. They may also be omitted.

We eat stewed peaches, sliced bananas, chutney and rice with the bobotie.

    1 slice white bread, 2,5 cm thick
    375 ml milk (1½ c)
    2 medium onions
    30 ml butter/margarine (2 T)
    25 ml medium curry powder (5 t)
    4 eggs
    1 kg minced beef
    30 ml lemon juice (2 T)
    15 ml sugar (1 T)
    7 ml salt (1½ t)
    5 lemon leaves

Preheat the oven to 180 °C. Soak the bread in the milk.

Peel the onions and chop them roughly. Lightly sauté the onions in the butter/margarine. Stir in the curry powder and fry lightly with the onions.

Press most of the milk out of the bread (reserve the milk) and crumble the bread. Beat one of the eggs.

Mix the bread, beaten egg, curried onions, minced beef, lemon juice, sugar and salt. Spoon the mince mixture into an ovenproof dish with a volume of about 2,5 litres (10 c). Roll up the lemon leaves and insert them in the mixture.

Beat together the remaining eggs and milk and pour it over the meat mixture.

Bake the bobotie for about 1¼ hours till golden brown and done. Serve hot.

Makes 6 servings

FREEZER MEAT PATTIES

These patties simplify life if you freeze them uncooked for later use. They make tasty food for a long journey and are very good in a hamburger roll or pita bread.

500 g pork sausage
500 g lean minced beef
1 slice white bread, 4 cm thick
1 large onion
125 ml milk (½ c)
1 egg
7 ml salt (1½ t)
2 ml dried mixed herbs (½ t)
pinch of pepper
cake flour
sunflower oil

Remove the pork sausage meat from the casings. Add the minced beef and mix lightly with a fork.

Crumble the white bread. Peel the onion and chop finely. Beat together the milk, egg, salt, mixed herbs and pepper.

Lightly mix the meat, breadcrumbs, onion and milk mixture with a fork. Shape meat patties from the mixture – each patty being 140 g (½ c) meat mixture, 8–9 cm in diameter and about 2,5 cm thick.

Dust the patties on both sides with cake flour. Place the patties between layers of waxed paper or aluminium foil in a freezer container and freeze.

To cook: Thaw as many patties as needed and fry over moderate heat in shallow sunflower oil till brown and done.

Makes 10 large patties

SCRUMPTIOUS HAMBURGER SAUCE

Cook the following ingredients together for 5 minutes: 200 ml (¾ c) each of finely chopped lettuce and fried onions, 125 ml (½ c) each of mayonnaise, chutney and tomato sauce, about 30 ml (2 T) prepared mustard and 15 ml (1 T) Worcestershire sauce. Leave to cool.

CREOLE CHICKEN CASSEROLE

The Creole descendants of European colonists in Latin America have developed a distinctive and very flavourful style of cooking. Tomatoes, green peppers and rice are characteristic ingredients in their recipes – as in this dish. The chicken may be replaced with portions of boerewors.

200 g rice (1 c)
1 kg chicken portions
salt and pepper
125 ml sunflower oil (½ c)
1 medium green pepper
1 medium onion
2 cloves garlic
1 tin (400 g) whole peeled tomatoes
2 ml curry powder (½ t)
2 ml dried thyme (½ t)

Cook the rice in the usual way until almost done. Rinse in a colander under cold running water and drain.

Season the chicken portions with salt and pepper. Heat the oil in a heavy-based saucepan. Quickly fry a couple of chicken portions at a time in the oil until golden brown on both sides. Place chicken in a shallow, ovenproof dish with a volume of 2,5 litres (10 c). Sprinkle the rice on top.

Halve and seed the green pepper and cut it in strips. Peel the onion and chop roughly. Peel and crush the garlic. Place in the pot in which the chicken was fried. (Leave just enough oil in the pot to braise the vegetables.) Cut the tomatoes into pieces and add together with the juice, curry powder and thyme. Cover with a lid and braise the vegetables for 10 minutes. Season with salt and pepper.

Spoon the vegetables over the rice layer. Cover the container. Cook the dish for about 40 minutes at 200 °C until the chicken is tender. Serve with young peas and a beetroot salad.

Makes 6 servings

HELEN'S CHICKEN AND VEGETABLE BAKE

My four Human aunts were all excellent cooks and were never mean about sharing their recipes. My first cookbook bears witness to this, as every other recipe bears the name of Helen, Baby, Letta or Marie.

CHICKEN
1 large chicken
70 g cake flour (½ c)
5 ml chicken spice (1 t)
5 ml salt (1 t)
1 ml pepper (¼ t)
sunflower oil

VEGETABLES
1 large potato
1 large carrot
250 g mushrooms
125 g green peas (1 c)
2 bay leaves
1 chicken stock cube
125 ml boiling water (½ c)

Preheat the oven to 180 °C.

Cut the chicken into portions. Mix the cake flour, chicken spice, salt and pepper and roll the chicken portions in the mixture. Fry the chicken portions quickly in hot sunflower oil till golden brown.

Peel the potato and carrot and dice. Wipe the mushrooms with a damp cloth and slice them. Mix the potato, carrot, mushrooms and green peas. Arrange the chicken and vegetables in layers in an ovenproof dish. (I rather like making this dish in a Römertopf.) Add the bay leaves. Dissolve the chicken stock cube in the boiling water. Pour the stock over the chicken and cover the dish.

Cook the chicken for about 30 minutes at 180 °C and then for one hour at 160 °C. Serve the chicken hot with rice.

Makes 6–8 servings

FRIED CHICKEN PORTIONS

If you make this treat at home, you can be selective and choose just those cuts of chicken preferred by your family – say, thighs and wings.

    1,5 kg chicken portions
    250 ml water (1 c)
    7 ml salt (1½ t)
    140 g cake flour (1 c)
    5 ml baking powder (1 t)
    5 ml chicken spice (1 t)
    pinch of pepper
    1 egg
    sunflower oil

Simmer the chicken portions for about half an hour in the water to which 5 ml (1 t) of the salt has been added. Drain the chicken portions, but reserve 200 ml (¾ c) of the liquid. (If there is less, add some milk.) Leave the chicken portions and the liquid to cool, but do not allow the liquid to set. Sift the remaining 2 ml (½ t) salt, the cake flour, baking powder, chicken spice and pepper. Beat together the egg and the chicken liquid. Blend the egg mixture with the flour mixture.

Dip the chicken portions in the batter. Fry four portions at a time in moderately hot deep sunflower oil till golden brown and done. Drain the cooked chicken on paper towelling and keep hot.

Makes 4–6 servings

OVEN-FRIED CHICKEN

Wash the chicken portions and dry with paper towelling. Season with salt and pepper and dip each portion in melted butter/margarine. Then roll the chicken portions in cornflake crumbs to which a little Parmesan cheese has been added. Place the portions in a greased ovenproof dish and trickle melted butter/margarine on top. Bake the portions uncovered for about an hour at 160 °C until tender.

MARINATED CHICKEN

If you are planning a meal in the garden, cook this chicken slowly over the coals in an old-fashioned plough disk. Do serve this dish with rice as it has plenty of gravy.

1 large chicken
1 tin (410 g) apricot halves
2 large onions
125 ml Worcestershire sauce (½ c)
60 ml brown vinegar (¼ c)
60 ml sunflower oil (¼ c)
50 g sugar (4 T)
15 ml soya sauce (1 T)
10 ml salt (2 t)
5 ml mustard powder (1 t)
5 ml paprika (1 t)
15 ml cornflour (1 T)

Cut the chicken into portions. Drain the apricots and supplement the syrup with water to make 250 ml (1 c).

Peel the onions. Grate one of them coarsely and slice the other one.

Mix the grated onion with the watered syrup, Worcestershire sauce, brown vinegar, sunflower oil, sugar, soya sauce, salt, mustard powder and paprika.

Layer the chicken portions in a deep glass or plastic container and spoon some of the marinade over every layer. Arrange the onion slices on top of the chicken portions. Cover the dish. Marinate the chicken overnight in the refrigerator.

Next day stew the chicken portions in the marinade in a heavy-based saucepan until tender. Remove the chicken from the marinade and place the apricot halves between the portions of chicken.

Spoon the oil off the sauce. Mix the cornflour to a paste with a little water and thicken the gravy with it. Spoon some of the gravy over the chicken portions and apricot halves and heat the dish through. Serve the remaining gravy separately in a gravy boat with the chicken.

Makes 6 servings

LIGHT MEALS

One-dish meals, such as a savoury pasta dish, make quite a pleasant change, as they not only ensure variety but save a lot of time too. It's much quicker to make a single-dish meal than to cook a whole variety of dishes. And there is also less to wash up afterwards! Everyone loves dishes like savoury tart, macaroni and cheese, pizza and curried eggs. They are also wonderful dishes to eat in front of the TV.

SAVOURY TART

Our family has been using this recipe for donkey's years. This savoury tart is not only mouthwatering, but it is also very simple to make. I make it quite regularly and I've never come across anyone who didn't ask for seconds.

CRUST
140 g cake flour (1 c)
5 ml baking powder (1 t)
2 ml salt (½ t)
50 g butter/margarine (4 T)
15 ml sunflower oil (1 T)
1 egg

FILLING
15 ml butter/margarine (1 T)
15 ml cake flour (1 T)
2 ml salt (½ t)
250 ml milk (1 c)
5 ml dried parsley (1 t)
2 ml mustard powder (½ t)
pinch of pepper
5 eggs
1 large onion
30 ml sunflower oil (2 T)
1 tin (385 g) smoked Vienna sausages
100 g coarsely grated Cheddar cheese (1 c)
5 ml tomato sauce (1 t)

Sift together the cake flour, the baking powder and the salt. Rub in the butter/margarine. Beat together the sunflower oil and the egg and combine the egg mixture with the flour mixture to form a dough. Cover and leave to rest for a while.

Make a white sauce from the butter/margarine, flour, salt and milk. Season it with the parsley, mustard powder and pepper. Leave to cool.

Hard-boil three of the eggs, shell them and grate coarsely. Beat the other two eggs into the white sauce.

Peel the onion and chop roughly. Sauté the onion in the sunflower oil. Drain the Vienna sausages and slice. Mix the white sauce mixture with the grated eggs, onion, sausages and cheese.

Preheat the oven to 180 °C. Press the dough thinly into an ovenproof pie dish with a volume of about 1,25 litres (5 c). Spoon the filling into the raw crust. Dot the top with the tomato sauce.

Bake the tart for about 40 minutes until it is done and starting to brown on top.

Serve the tart lukewarm.

Makes 4–6 servings

LIGHT MEALS 67

MARTJIE'S MACARONI

Aunt Martjie and uncle Driesie van der Westhuizen kept open house in their spacious home in Melville, Johannesburg, and no one ever left hungry or thirsty. Aunt Martjie was a busy little woman who was always laughing. And could she cook! Here is one of her never-fail dishes.

- 250 g macaroni pieces (2 c)
- 20 ml salt (4 t)
- 1,5 litres boiling water (6 c)
- 1 large onion
- 250 g finely sliced celery (2½ c)
- 50 g butter/margarine (4 T)
- 150 g coarsely grated Cheddar cheese (1½ c)
- 100 g fresh breadcrumbs (1½ c)
- 1 litre milk (4 c)
- 3 extra large eggs

Preheat the oven to 180 °C. Grease a shallow ovenproof dish with a volume of about 2,5 litres (10 c).

Cook the macaroni, 15 ml (1 T) of the salt and the boiling water for 12 minutes until the macaroni is done, but still firm (the culinary term is 'al dente'). Drain the macaroni and rinse it in a colander under cold running water.

Peel the onion and chop roughly. Sauté the onion and the celery in the butter/margarine. Mix lightly with the macaroni, cheese and breadcrumbs. Spoon the mixture into the dish.

Beat together the milk, the eggs and the remaining 5 ml (1 t) salt. Pour the milk mixture over the macaroni mixture.

Bake uncovered for about an hour until set and done. Leave to stand for a few minutes before serving.

Makes 6–8 servings

MONDAY MACARONI CHEESE

This recipe has developed over the years. I usually make it on a Monday when I have to attend to a thousand things and do not have much time for cooking. I serve it with a tomato salad and crisp lettuce leaves. My husband, who has a decidedly sweet tooth, trickles golden syrup over his helping.

- 250 g macaroni pieces (2 c)
- 20 ml salt (4 t)
- 1,5 litres boiling water (6 c)
- 200 g coarsely grated Cheddar cheese (2 c)
- 30 ml cornflour (2 T)
- 1 litre milk (4 c)
- 5 extra large eggs
- 5 ml mustard powder (1 t)
- pinch of pepper

Preheat the oven to 180 °C. Grease a shallow ovenproof dish with a volume of about 2,5 litres (10 c).

Cook the macaroni, 15 ml (1 T) of the salt and the boiling water for 12 minutes, until the macaroni is done, but still firm. Drain the macaroni. Layer the macaroni and the cheese in the dish. End with a layer of cheese.

Mix the cornflour with a little of the milk and then add to the remaining milk. Beat together with the eggs, the remaining 5 ml (1 t) salt, mustard powder and pepper till mixed. Pour the egg mixture over the macaroni and cheese.

Bake the dish uncovered for an hour until done and nicely browned on top.

Makes 6–8 servings

TASTY TOMATO SALAD

Cut well-ripened tomatoes into thin slices. Layer with finely chopped onion and shredded fresh basil in a salad bowl. Sprinkle salt, pepper and a touch of sugar over each layer.

WHOLEWHEAT PIZZA

If you have any fresh herbs growing in your garden, chop them finely and sprinkle them over the raw pizza just before popping it into the oven. Origanum, marjoram, thyme, basil or parsley are all a good choice and any one of them will add that special something to the pizza.

CRUST
260 g wholewheat flour (2 c)
10 ml baking powder (2 t)
5 ml salt (1 t)
125 ml boiling water (½ c)
125 ml sunflower oil (½ c)

FILLING
2 ripe medium tomatoes
1 medium onion
2 rashers bacon
1 tin (200 g) tuna, canned in oil
salt and pepper
50 g coarsely grated Cheddar cheese (½ c)

Preheat the oven to 200 °C. Grease an ovenproof pizza plate measuring about 30 cm in diameter.

Mix the flour, baking powder and salt in a plastic container with a tight-fitting lid. Add the boiling water and sunflower oil. Put on the lid and shake the container until a loose dough has formed. Press the dough into the pizza plate.

Peel the tomatoes and onion. Chop roughly. Cut the bacon into pieces. Drain the tuna and reserve the oil.

Fry the bacon in the tuna oil. Remove the bacon from the pan and then fry the tomatoes and onion in the same oil until the mixture is fairly dry.

Spread the tomato and onion mixture over the crust. Season with salt and pepper. Roughly flake the tuna and sprinkle over the crust together with the bacon. Sprinkle the cheese on top.

Bake the pizza for about 20 minutes till slightly brown. Serve piping hot.

Makes 6 servings

CURRIED EGGS

Come summer or winter, curried eggs served with chutney and a large bowl of salad is a popular supper in our home.

A fried egg on a slice of buttered toast with a little of this sauce on top is a succulent breakfast snack.

6 eggs
200 g rice (1 c)
5 ml salt (1 t)

SAUCE
1 large onion
1 medium carrot
1 medium apple
30 ml sunflower oil (2 T)
10 ml medium curry powder (2 t)
2 ml turmeric (½ t)
50 g sugar (4 T)
30 g cake flour (3 T)
5 ml salt (1 t)
60 ml brown vinegar (¼ c)
500 ml chicken stock (2 c)

Hard-boil the eggs. Shell them and halve each one lengthwise. Boil the rice in plenty of water until the grains are done but not mushy. Drain the rice well and stir in the salt. Spoon the rice into a serving platter and keep it hot.

Peel the onion, carrot and apple. Chop the onion finely and roughly grate the carrot and apple. Sauté in the sunflower oil. Add the curry powder and turmeric and fry the mixture lightly.

Mix the sugar, cake flour and salt. Mix to a paste with the brown vinegar. Add the paste and chicken stock to the onion mixture and mix. Bring the sauce to the boil. Boil uncovered for a few minutes over moderate heat.

Spoon the hot curry sauce over the rice and arrange the eggs on top. Serve the dish immediately.

Makes 4–6 servings

PUDDINGS

Nothing rounds off a meal more satisfyingly than a good pudding. Ask those with a sweet tooth what their favourite puddings are and you will soon discover how many scrumptious puddings there are to choose from – old-fashioned sago pudding, rice dumplings, toffee bread pudding, home-made ice cream, chocolate delight. Here are some pudding recipes that are always in demand, whether it's winter or summer.

PANCAKES WITH RHUBARB FILLING

My rhubarb plant is flourishing in the shade of a wild fig in Hoogland's garden. It's not only lovely to look at, but also delicious to eat.

After often hearing how marvellous rhubarb tastes with pancakes, my mother-in-law taught me how to make this pudding. Sometimes I vary the recipe by replacing this rhubarb filling with a filling of stewed, puréed guavas.

BATTER
140 g cake flour (1 c)
5 ml baking powder (1 t)
1 ml salt (¼ t)
250 ml milk (1 c)
250 ml water (1 c)
1 egg
30 ml sunflower oil (2 T)

FILLING
750 g rhubarb stalks
250 g sugar (1¼ c)

Sift together the flour, baking powder and salt. Beat together the milk, water, egg and sunflower oil. Add the milk mixture to the flour mixture and beat until mixed. Chill the batter for an hour.

Pull the skin off the rhubarb stalks. Cut into lengths of 2,5 cm. Place the rhubarb in a stainless steel or enamelled saucepan and cover with cold water. Bring just to the boil and drain.

Add the sugar to the rhubarb and cook over low heat till somewhat dry, but watch out for burning. (Taste and add more sugar if necessary.)

Fry smallish pancakes from the batter in the usual way. Put just enough sunflower oil in the pan to coat the base lightly before frying each pancake.

To serve: Place a pancake in a pudding dish or bowl, spoon some of the filling over the pancake and serve the dessert with cream or ice cream.

Makes approximately 8 servings

THE ORIGIN OF RHUBARB
The word rhubarb is probably derived from 'rha', the Greek word for Volga, and 'barbarus', the Latin for a barbarian. It was apparently brought from Russia to the West for the first time in about 1580, as a decorative garden plant.

PUDDINGS 73

ORANGE PUDDING

To make this pudding, the batter is baked in a luscious orange syrup. This causes a thick layer of custard to form on the bottom of the dish with a delicious layer of cake on top. We usually eat this simple but very palatable pudding with ice cream or a thin custard sauce.

BATTER
100 g sugar (½ c)
50 g butter/margarine (4 T)
1 extra large egg
15 ml smooth apricot jam (1 T)
2 ml finely grated orange rind (½ t)
2 ml bicarbonate of soda (½ t)
125 ml milk (½ c)
100 g cake flour (¾ c)

SYRUP
250 ml orange juice (1 c)
50 g sugar (4 T)
15 ml butter/margarine (1 T)
1 ml salt (¼ t)

Preheat the oven to 190 °C.

Cream the sugar, butter/margarine, egg, apricot jam and orange rind. Dissolve the bicarbonate of soda in the milk. Add the soda milk and cake flour alternately to the sugar mixture, mixing well.

Bring all the syrup ingredients to the boil in a saucepan on the stove or in a microwave dish at 100% power in the microwave oven. Stir occasionally.

Pour the boiling syrup into a deep ovenproof dish with a volume of about 1,5 litres (6 c). Spoon the batter carefully into the hot syrup.

Bake the pudding for about 20 minutes till it is golden brown and done. Serve the pudding lukewarm.

Makes 4–6 servings

TOFFEE BREAD PUDDING

It's not easy to find a recipe for a pudding made in a frying pan. Remember this recipe when next you go camping and feel an inclination for pudding. Everything is quite simply done in a frying pan – it's almost as easy as frying eggs.

The buttermilk combines very well with the toffee sauce in which the bread is fried.

    3 slices white bread, each
      2,5 cm thick
    200 ml milk (¾ c)
    1 egg
    80 g butter/margarine (6 T)
    80 g sugar (5 T)
    100 ml golden syrup (6 T)
    125 ml buttermilk (½ c)

Cut the crusts off the bread. Cut each slice into quarters. Beat the milk and the egg.

Melt half of the butter/margarine in a large heavy-based frying pan over moderate heat. Add half of the sugar and half of the golden syrup. Stir the sugar mixture till the grains of sugar are dissolved and the mixture begins to boil.

Dip the quarters of bread in the egg and milk mixture and place them in the hot toffee syrup. Fry each piece till golden brown on one side, and then fry on the other side. Carefully remove the quarters of bread from the pan.

Make more syrup from the remaining butter/margarine, sugar and golden syrup.

Place half the fried bread quarters in a serving dish. Pour half of the buttermilk over the bread, and then half of the toffee syrup. Repeat the layers.

Serve immediately.

Makes 6 servings

BAKED SAGO PUDDING

When my aunt Baby came to visit us from the Cape, all the ladies decided to travel from Pretoria to Rustenburg to go and visit my aunt Bets.

Halfway to Rustenburg we stopped the car under a tree along the roadside at Mooinooi to have tea and a slice of my mother's coconut cake.

When we arrived at Rustenburg, aunt Bets wasn't there. So we had a picnic in her garden under the giant old acacia tree and summarily polished off the whole dish of sago pudding that we had brought for her. What a wonderful memory!

- 2 litres milk (8 c)
- 160 g sago (¾ c)
- 2 ml salt (½ t)
- 150 g sugar (¾ c)
- 125 g butter/margarine
- 6 extra large eggs
- 5 ml vanilla essence (1 t)
- 1 ml ground nutmeg (¼ t)

Bring the milk to the boil in a heavy-based saucepan. Add the sago and salt and cook uncovered over very low heat until it looks like thick custard and the sago is transparent. Stir regularly.

Preheat the oven to 160 °C. Grease a shallow ovenproof dish with a volume of approximately 2,5 litres (10 c).

Stir the sugar and the butter/margarine into the sago mixture in the saucepan. Remove the saucepan from the stove.

Beat the eggs with the vanilla essence. Using a wire whisk, beat the egg mixture quickly into the hot sago mixture. Pour into the dish. Sift the nutmeg over the top.

Place the dish in a larger ovenproof dish or roasting pan containing hot water.

Bake the pudding for about 90 minutes till set and golden brown on top.

Makes 12–15 servings

RICE DUMPLINGS

It's my mother's fault that we like rice dumplings so much, because she often made them for us. The big secret of rice dumplings is to cook them in shallow, slowly simmering water. If there's too much water, or if it boils too fast, you end up with a mushy mess. I sometimes flavour the rice mixture with a pinch of nutmeg.

> 300 g cooked rice (2 c)
> 50 g cake flour (5½ T)
> 10 ml baking powder (2 t)
> 5 ml salt (1 t)
> 2 extra large eggs
> cinnamon sugar
> 30 ml butter/margarine (2 T)

Mix the rice, cake flour, baking powder and half the salt. Beat the eggs and stir into the rice mixture.

Pour boiling water about 1 cm deep into a large frying pan with a lid. Let the water simmer very slowly. Spoon dessertspoons of the rice mixture into the boiling water. Put on the lid and simmer the dumplings for about 7 minutes. Spoon the dumplings into a shallow dish, sprinkle with cinnamon sugar and keep hot.

Supplement the water in the pan to a depth of 1 cm before cooking the next batch of dumplings.

When all the dumplings have been cooked, add a little extra boiling water and the remaining salt to the water in which the dumplings were cooked. Melt the butter/margarine in the water and sweeten to taste with a little cinnamon sugar. Pour some of this sauce over the dumplings in the dish and serve the rest separately with the dumplings.

Makes 6 servings

78 PUDDINGS

BAKED APPLE DUMPLINGS

You can use any kind of apple for these ... and should the apples be slightly past their prime, it doesn't matter.

> 275 g cake flour (2 c)
> 15 ml sugar (1 T)
> 2 ml baking powder (½ t)
> 2 ml salt (½ t)
> 175 g butter/margarine (¾ c)
> 1 egg
> 50 ml water (3 T)
> 6 smallish apples
> 40 g seedless raisins (4 T)
> cinnamon sugar
> lemon juice

Sift together the cake flour, sugar, baking powder and salt. Rub in the butter/margarine. Separate the egg. Beat the egg yolk and water till just mixed. Gradually cut it into the flour mixture. Press the mixture together to form a dough. Cover the dough and leave to rest for a while.

Preheat the oven to about 180 °C. Peel and core the apples.

Divide the dough into six equal pieces. Roll each piece out thinly on a floured pastry board and cut out a circle 18 cm in diameter. Place an apple on each circle. Fill the hollow of each apple with raisins, sprinkle with cinnamon sugar and trickle a little lemon juice over each apple.

Lightly beat the egg white. Brush the edge of the pastry circle with it. Fold the pastry around the apple and press it together at the top. Roll out the scraps of dough and cut out any shape. Attach to the apple with egg white.

Place the apples a little distance apart in an ovenproof dish. Brush with milk and sprinkle with a little sugar if you like.

Bake the apples for about 40 minutes until done and nicely browned on top.

Makes 6 servings

APPLE BREAD PUDDING

When it's apple season, we always buy a good few boxes of apples at Ceres for the winter months in the Bushveld, because when it's cold, I like to make this simple but scrumptious hot pudding. Any kind of apples may be used.

> 1 kg apples
> 8 thin slices white bread
> butter/margarine
> 50 g cinnamon sugar (4 T)
> 2 eggs
> 250 ml milk (1 c)
> 40 g castor sugar (3 T)
> 1 ml cream of tartar (¼ t)

Cut the apples in quarters and core. Peel the quarters and cut up. Place the apple pieces in a large pan or saucepan, put on the lid and cook over moderate heat till done. Stir at regular intervals and towards the end, crush into smaller pieces.

Remove the crusts from the bread. Spread each slice with butter/margarine. Place half the slices, buttered side down, in a square or rectangular ovenproof dish with a volume of 2 litres (8 c). Spread half of the cooked apple on top. Sprinkle half of the cinnamon sugar over the apple. Repeat the layers with the remaining slices of bread, apple and cinnamon sugar.

Separate the eggs. Beat the milk and egg yolks. Pour the milk mixture over the mixture in the dish and leave to stand.

Preheat the oven to 160 °C. Bake the pudding uncovered for 30 minutes.

Beat the egg whites till frothy. Beat in the castor sugar a little at a time. Add the cream of tartar and beat the meringue till it is thick and shiny. Spread the meringue over the hot pudding.

Lower the oven temperature to 140 °C. Bake uncovered for another half an hour.

Makes 6–8 servings

STEAMED FRUIT PUDDING

This pudding is definitely a winner for special occasions.

If you don't own a steaming pot, you can steam it in a deep 2 litre mixing bowl. Cover securely with aluminium foil before placing it in the large saucepan.

SAUCE
10 glacé cherries
250 ml water (1 c)
200 g sugar (1 c)
125 ml white vinegar (½ c)
30 ml each sultanas, currants and mixed peel (2 T each)

BATTER
230 g butter/margarine (1 c)
30 ml smooth apricot jam (2 T)
250 ml milk (1 c)
1 egg
10 ml bicarbonate of soda (2 t)
1 ml salt (¼ t)
275 g cake flour (2 c)

Halve the glacé cherries. Add the water, together with the sugar, vinegar, sultanas, currants and mixed peel and then heat the mixture until the sugar has just dissolved. Leave the sauce to cool.

Cream the butter/margarine and apricot jam. Beat the milk together with the egg, bicarbonate of soda and the salt. Stir the milk mixture and cake flour alternately into the creamed mixture.

Grease a steaming pot with a tight-fitting lid and a volume of 2 litres (8 c). Pour the sauce into the pot and arrange the fruit over the base of the pot. Carefully spoon the batter into the sauce. Seal the pot. Set it on an inverted saucer or wire stand in a large saucepan filled a third with boiling water. Put on the lid of the large saucepan. Steam the pudding for approximately 2½ hours over moderate heat. Add boiling water from time to time.

Invert the pudding carefully onto a serving dish and serve hot with custard.

Makes 8 servings

FESTIVAL MERINGUE

This is a magnificent dessert and just the thing for entertaining.

>   100 g cream crackers (½ packet)
>   3 extra large eggs
>   400 g sugar (2 c)
>   5 ml baking powder (1 t)
>   30 ml cornflour (2 T)
>   juice and finely grated rind of 2 ripe medium lemons
>   50 g butter/margarine (4 T)
>   1 tin (440 g) pineapple pieces
>   250 ml cream (1 c)
>   30 ml castor sugar (2 T)

Preheat the oven to 120 °C. Line a large baking sheet with aluminium foil. Draw two circles, each 20 cm in diameter, on the foil with a skewer. Grease the foil.

Break the cream crackers into pieces – do not crush. Separate the eggs. Beat the egg whites until stiff. Gradually beat in 200 g (1 c) of the sugar and keep beating until it becomes a shiny, thick meringue. Lightly fold in the pieces of cracker and then the baking powder.

Spread the meringue over the circles, evenly but not too smoothly. Bake for 2 hours till dry. Switch off the oven and leave to cool in the oven.

Mix the cornflour with the lemon juice. Add the remaining 200 g (1 c) sugar and the egg yolks and beat till well blended. Add the lemon rind and butter/margarine. Heat the mixture in the top of a double boiler over boiling water and stir every few minutes until after 15 minutes it is thick and cooked. Chill the lemon curd till it is ice cold.

Drain the pineapple pieces and chop finely. Beat the cream till thick and stir in the castor sugar. Fold in the pineapple.

Spoon half the lemon curd onto a meringue layer. Pile half of the pineapple cream on top. Repeat the layers. Chill the dessert before serving.

Makes 8–10 servings

LUSCIOUS LAYER PUDDING

This pudding can be served simply with canned fruit and custard, or it can be varied in a number of ways if you want something a little different.

For example, a small quantity of chopped nuts added to the crumbs makes the pudding taste extra good. Or what about banana slices or a little granadilla pulp added to the condensed milk mixture for a different taste? You can also make different colours of jelly, allow it to set, chop it up with a fork and arrange it in layers with the crumb and condensed milk mixtures in the pudding dish.

    1 packet (200 g) Tennis biscuits
    100 g coconut (1 c)
    30 ml soft brown sugar (2 T)
    15 ml finely grated lemon rind (1 T)
    115 g butter/margarine (½ c)
    1 tin (397 g) condensed milk
    125 ml lemon juice (½ c)
    250 ml cream (1 c)

Crumble the Tennis biscuits, but not too finely. (I usually put the biscuits into a strong plastic bag and crush them with a rolling pin on a pastry board.) Toast the coconut till it is golden brown.

Mix the biscuit crumbs, coconut, brown sugar and lemon rind. Melt the butter/margarine and mix it thoroughly with the crumb mixture.

Beat together the condensed milk and the lemon juice. Beat the cream until it just becomes stiff and fold it lightly into the condensed milk mixture.

Spoon the crumb and condensed milk mixtures alternately in layers in a pudding bowl or individual dishes. Start with a crumb layer and end with a layer of the condensed milk mixture. Decorate the top as you like and chill before serving.

Makes 6 servings

CHOCOLATE DELIGHT

In my recipe book, this dessert is called the Mrs Raubenheimer pudding. I actually never knew her, but her husband was one of the bank managers during my childhood in Rustenburg.

On special occasions, I decorate the pudding with chocolate leaves and a sprinkling of brown sugar.

To make chocolate leaves, cover the back of strong leaves, such as those of roses or other climbers, with melted chocolate and leave them to dry completely on waxed paper. Peel the leaves off very carefully when the chocolate has set.

1 tin (410 g) evaporated milk
15 ml gelatine (1 T)
60 ml water (¼ c)
150 g sugar (¾ c)
30 ml cocoa (2 T)
30 ml roughly grated ginger preserve (2 T)
15 ml ginger preserve syrup (1 T)

Boil the tin of evaporated milk in plenty of water for half an hour. Cool and chill overnight in the refrigerator or for an hour or two in the freezer till well chilled.

Soak the gelatine in the water and then clarify it over boiling water.

Quickly beat the evaporated milk to a thick froth. Mix the sugar and cocoa and beat gradually into the evaporated milk. Beat in the ginger preserve and the ginger syrup and then the gelatine. The gelatine should be gradually trickled in and beaten very quickly, so that it doesn't form lumps when it comes into contact with the cold evaporated milk mixture.

Spoon the mixture into a big glass dish and chill until set. Decorate according to personal taste and serve with custard.

Makes 8 servings

BANANA PUDDING

When I make this pudding, everyone always asks for seconds – and they protest if I give them too little. It is a very popular dessert in our family.

   3 extra large eggs
750 ml milk (3 c)
30 g cornflour (3 T)
pinch of salt
100 g sugar (½ c)
100 g Marie or Tennis biscuits
   (½ packet)
125 ml smooth apricot jam (½ c)
15 ml lemon juice (1 T)
4 ripe bananas
toasted coconut

Separate the eggs. Beat together the egg yolks, milk, cornflour, salt and half the sugar until well blended. Bring the milk mixture to the boil over moderate heat and stir continuously until a thick custard has formed. Leave to cool slightly.

Break the biscuits into pieces. Mix half of the apricot jam with the lemon juice. Add the jam mixture to the biscuits and mix lightly. Spoon half the mixture onto the base of a shallow pudding dish with a volume of approximately 1,5 litres (6 c). Spoon half the custard over the crust. Peel the bananas. Slice half of the bananas over the custard layer. Spread the rest of the biscuits on top of the bananas. Cover with the remaining custard and slice the rest of the bananas on top.

Beat the egg whites until they are very stiff. Beat the rest of the sugar into the egg whites and then beat in the remaining apricot jam. Pile the meringue on top of the last layer of bananas. Sprinkle the pudding with a little coconut and chill it very well before serving.

Makes 6–8 servings

CARAMEL COTTAGE CHEESE ICE CREAM

When I have fresh cream at my disposal at Hoogland, I always have this ice cream in the freezer. Sometimes I chop up pieces of watermelon preserve and stir it in.

2 eggs
150 g sugar (¾ c)
250 g smooth cottage cheese
500 ml cream (2 c)
200 ml milk (¾ c)
1 packet (90 g) caramel instant pudding

Beat the eggs and sugar until thick and creamy. Add the cottage cheese and mix. Beat together the cream, milk and instant pudding and add to the egg mixture. Pour the mixture into freezer containers and freeze until it starts to stiffen. Beat well with a fork and freeze till hard.

Makes about 1,75 litres (7 c) ice cream

SIMPLE VANILLA ICE CREAM

This is my basic ice cream recipe, because it's so simple to make and can be varied in many delicious ways. You can add just about anything, such as toasted coconut, glacé cherries soaked in brandy, grated chocolate or chopped canned fruit.

2 eggs
150 g sugar (¾ c)
500 ml cream (2 c)
450 ml milk (1¾ c)
10 ml vanilla essence (2 t)

Beat the eggs and sugar until thick and creamy. Add the cream, milk and vanilla essence and mix.
 Pour the mixture into freezer containers and freeze until it starts to stiffen. Beat the ice cream well with a fork and freeze again until hard.

Makes about 1 litre (4 c) ice cream

TARTS

When friends are coming to tea, the first question you ask yourself is: What shall I make to serve with the tea? What about a tart? There are thousands to choose from. Let the season influence your choice. Just think how glorious a chilled cheesecake or a cool, fresh lemon chiffon tart would taste on a hot summer's day, while in winter your guests would surely prefer a Cape brandy tart.

JEWISH TART

Jewish tart consists of thin rounds of shortcrust pastry layered with a milk filling. It is a special treat on the tea table.

FILLING
50 g cornflour (5½ T)
950 ml milk (3¾ c)
100 g sugar (½ c)
3 extra large egg yolks
5 ml vanilla essence (1 t)

PASTRY ROUNDS
75 g castor sugar (6 T)
40 g butter/margarine (3 T)
3 extra large egg whites
230 g cake flour (1¾ c)
15 ml baking powder (1 T)
1 ml salt (¼ t)

Mix the cornflour to a paste with a little of the milk. Stir it into the remaining milk. Add the sugar and egg yolks and beat till mixed. Stir the mixture over moderate heat until it thickens and comes to the boil. Stir in the vanilla essence. Cover the filling with a piece of wet waxed paper and cool at room temperature.

Preheat the oven to 180 °C. Invert cake pans with a diameter of 20 cm, so that the bases face upwards. Grease the bases.

Cream the castor sugar and the butter/margarine together. Add the egg whites and beat till mixed.

Sift together the cake flour, baking powder and salt. Add to the egg white mixture and mix to form a soft dough.

Divide the dough into 5 equal pieces. Thinly roll each piece of dough over an inverted pan. Cut the edge neatly and reserve the leftover pieces of dough.

Bake the pastry rounds and scraps of dough for about 6 minutes until they begin to change colour. Carefully loosen each crust from the base of the pan and cool on a wire rack. (The crusts are brittle and break easily.)

Divide the filling into 5 equal quantities. Place a pastry round on a serving platter and spoon a portion of filling over the pastry. Repeat with the remaining pastry rounds and filling. Crumble the remaining scraps of pastry and sprinkle on top.

Refrigerate overnight in a closed container before cutting.

Makes a medium tart

TARTS 87

EASY MILK TART

This milk tart is mostly filling with just a hint of a crust. Mother Martie was the initiator of this almost-crust. She was already getting tired of this recipe, but all the children protested when she wanted to use another recipe.

    50 g Tennis or Marie biscuits (¼ packet)
    750 ml milk (3 c)
    115 g butter/margarine (½ c)
    100 g sugar (½ c)
    40 g cake flour (4 T)
    30 g cornflour (3 T)
    1 ml salt (¼ t)
    2 extra large eggs
    5 ml vanilla essence (1 t)
    30 ml coconut (2 T)
    cinnamon sugar

Preheat the oven to 180 °C. Grease an ovenproof pie dish with a volume of 1,25 litres (5 c) with butter/margarine.

Crumble the Tennis or Marie biscuits. Place the crumbs in the pie dish and shake to coat the base and sides.

Bring to the boil 625 ml (2½ c) of the milk, the butter/margarine and half the sugar. Mix the remaining sugar with the cake flour, cornflour and salt.

Separate the eggs. Beat together the egg yolks and the remaining 125 ml (½ c) milk, and combine this mixture with the flour mixture. Add a little of the boiling milk mixture to the flour mixture. Add the flour mixture to the remaining boiling milk mixture, stirring well. Bring to the boil slowly and stir continuously.

Remove the saucepan from the stove and stir in the vanilla essence. Beat the egg whites till soft peaks form. Fold lightly into the custard. Pour the filling into the crust. Sprinkle coconut on top.

Bake the tart for about half an hour until it starts to brown. Sprinkle a little cinnamon sugar on top. Serve lukewarm.

Makes a medium tart

ROSIE'S APPLE PIE

Rosie Pieterse was a matron of the girls' hostel at Rustenburg High School during the sixties. She was an excellent cook and this recipe for her apple pie is one of my all-time favourites.

When I don't have fresh apples, I use a medium tin of unsweetened pie apples.

For a nicely browned crust, I brush it with an egg yolk which has been beaten together with a little milk, and I also sprinkle a little sugar on top.

CRUST
200 g cake flour (1½ c)
7 ml baking powder (1½ t)
1 ml salt (¼ t)
125 g butter/margarine
60 ml cold water (¼ c)

FILLING
4 medium apples
50 g cinnamon sugar (4 T)
15 ml butter/margarine (1 T)

Sift together the cake flour, baking powder and salt. Rub in the butter/margarine. Sprinkle the water over the mixture and mix to form a dough. Place the dough in a plastic bag and leave to rest for a while.

Preheat the oven to 190 °C. Grease an ovenproof pie dish with a volume of about 1 litre (4 c).

Roll two-thirds of the dough out thinly and line the pie dish with it. Peel the apples, cut them in quarters and remove the cores. Coarsely grate the apples and place in the pastry crust. Sprinkle the cinnamon sugar on top of the apples and dot with the butter/margarine.

Roll out the remaining dough thinly. Moisten the edge of the pastry crust with water. Place the remaining dough over the filling and crust and press the edges together well. Trim neatly. Prick the upper crust with a fork.

Bake the pie for about 35 minutes till the crust is lightly browned.

Makes 6 servings

GREEK COCONUT TART

The combination of coconut and tangy orange juice in this moist, cake-like tart is quite irresistible. If you're lucky enough not to be overconcerned about kilojoules, serve it with beaten cream.

    125 g butter/margarine
    3 extra large eggs
    400 g sugar (2 c)
    250 ml orange juice (1 c)
    finely grated rind of 1 orange
    140 g cake flour (1 c)
    15 ml baking powder (1 T)
    1 ml salt (¼ t)
    160 g coconut (2 c)
    250 ml water (1 c)

Preheat the oven to 180 °C. Grease an ovenproof pie dish with a volume of about 1,5 litres (6 c).

Cream together the butter/margarine, eggs and half the sugar. Add the orange juice and rind and stir well.

Sift together the cake flour, baking powder and salt. Stir together with the coconut into the egg mixture. Spoon the batter into the pie dish. Bake the tart for 35 minutes until done and golden brown.

Boil the water and the remaining sugar uncovered for about 5 minutes. Pour the boiling syrup over the hot tart just after it has been taken from the oven.

Serve the tart lukewarm or cold.

Makes a medium tart

PRACTICAL COCONUT TARTS

One can vary this recipe in a practical way by baking the batter in muffin pans and decorating each individual tartlet with a rosette of cream.

One can do the same with the batter for Cape Brandy Tart.

CAPE BRANDY TART

Decorate the tart with stiffly beaten cream which has been slightly sweetened.

BATTER
250 g dates
5 ml bicarbonate of soda (1 t)
200 ml boiling water (¾ c)
100 g sugar (½ c)
30 ml butter/margarine (2 T)
1 extra large egg
180 g cake flour (1¼ c)
10 ml baking powder (2 t)
2 ml ground nutmeg (½ t)
1 ml salt (¼ t)
50 g chopped nuts (½ c)

SYRUP
200 g sugar (1 c)
125 ml water (½ c)
60 ml brandy (¼ c)
15 ml butter/margarine (1 T)
5 ml vanilla essence (1 t)
pinch of salt

Chop up the dates and remove stones if there are any. Sprinkle the dates with the bicarbonate of soda. Add the boiling water and leave the date mixture to cool for a while. Stir at regular intervals.

Preheat the oven to 190 °C. Grease an ovenproof pie dish with a volume of about 750 ml (3 c).

Beat the sugar, butter/margarine and egg together very well. Sift together the cake flour, baking powder, nutmeg and salt. Stir the flour mixture and the date mixture alternately into the egg mixture. Finally stir in the nuts. Spoon the mixture into the pie dish.

Bake the tart for about 30 minutes until done. Leave to cool for 10 minutes.

Boil the sugar and water for 5 minutes. Add the remaining syrup ingredients. Pour the syrup over the tart, a little at a time. Chill the tart until it is ice cold.

Makes a medium tart

LEMON CHIFFON TART

I am completely crazy about this tart. It's as light as the proverbial feather and has a mild lemon taste which is most refreshing. To make the tart even more attractive, I sometimes decorate it with stiffly beaten, sweetened cream.

CRUST
150 g Marie biscuits (¾ packet)
75 g butter/margarine (5½ T)

FILLING
5 ml gelatine (1 t)
50 ml water (3 T)
3 extra large eggs
150 g sugar (¾ c)
30 ml lemon juice (2 T)
finely grated rind of 1 lemon
pinch of salt

Crumble the Marie biscuits. Melt the butter/margarine and mix it with the crumbs. Reserve a little of the crumb mixture to sprinkle over the filling later. Using the back of a metal spoon, press the remaining crumbs firmly onto the sides and the base of a pie dish with a volume of about 1 litre (4 c).

Soak the gelatine in the water. Separate the eggs. Beat the egg yolks and half the sugar until well blended. Add the lemon juice, rind and salt and stir well. Stir the mixture in a double boiler over boiling water till it sticks to the spoon. Add the soaked gelatine to the mixture.

Beat the egg whites until they become frothy. Gradually beat in the remaining sugar. Keep beating until the meringue forms soft peaks. Fold the meringue lightly into the lemon mixture.

Spoon the lemon filling into the crust. Sprinkle the remaining crumbs on top. Chill the tart until it has set.

Makes a medium tart

CHEESECAKE

My variation of this very popular tart is made with a cornflake and coconut crust.

CRUST
80 g cornflakes (2 c)
50 g coconut (½ c)
40 g butter/margarine (3 T)
15 ml sugar (1 T)

FILLING
10 ml gelatine (2 t)
30 ml water (2 T)
125 ml condensed milk (½ c)
30 ml lemon juice (2 T)
1 container (250 g) smooth cottage cheese
125 ml cream (½ c)
125 ml smooth apricot jam (½ c)

Crush the cornflakes with a rolling pin. Toast the coconut until golden brown. Melt the butter/margarine. Mix the cornflakes, coconut, butter/margarine and sugar together well. Press firmly with the back of a metal spoon onto the sides and base of a pie dish with a volume of about 750 ml (3 c). Chill the crust.

Soak 5 ml (1 t) of the gelatine in 15 ml (1 T) of the water and clarify the soaked gelatine over boiling water.

Mix the condensed milk and lemon juice well. Add the cottage cheese and blend. Beat the cream till stiff. Fold the cream and the clarified gelatine into the cottage cheese mixture. Spoon the filling into the crust and chill till set.

Soak the remaining 5 ml (1 t) gelatine in the remaining 15 ml (1 T) water. Add the apricot jam to the soaked gelatine and heat until it is just warm. Pour the jam mixture over the back of a spoon onto the filling. Chill the tart until set.

Makes a medium tart

CARAMEL TART

This recipe started a couple of years ago with Ansie de Beer. One day she phoned: 'When you come to town, pop in for tea and I'll make a tart that you don't know at all.' Naturally I ate far too much of it and came home bearing Ansie's recipe. Today she is a minister's wife in the Northwest.

CRUST
150 g Marie or Tennis
  biscuits (¾ packet)
115 g butter/margarine (½ c)

FILLING
1 litre milk (4 c)
3 extra large eggs
150 g sugar (¾ c)
70 g cake flour (½ c)
30 g cornflour (3 T)
2 ml salt (½ t)
1 tin (380 g) caramel condensed milk
250 ml cream (1 c)
4 soft caramel sweets (optional)

Crumble the Marie or Tennis biscuits. Melt the butter/margarine and stir into the crumbs. Press the crumbs with the back of a metal spoon firmly onto the sides and the base of a pie dish with a volume of approximately 2 litres (8 c).

Bring to the boil 750 ml (3 c) of the milk. Separate the eggs. Beat the yolks with the remaining milk. Mix together the sugar, flour, cornflour and salt and mix with the egg yolk mixture (there must be no lumps). Beat quickly into the boiling milk and boil until thick, stirring often.

Beat the egg whites until they are stiff but not dry. Fold into the hot custard, using a metal spoon. Pour the filling into the crust and chill till set.

Beat the caramel condensed milk. Beat the cream till stiff. Fold 125 ml (½ c) of the caramel condensed milk into the cream and spread the rest over the filling. Cover with the cream mixture. Grate the caramel sweets roughly on top.

Makes a large tart

GINGER TART

This tart is positively mouthwatering and therefore it is easy to eat far too much of it. For this reason, I adapted the original recipe so that I could make two tarts at a time. It tastes so good that one tart is quite simply not enough!

CRUST
300 g Marie or Tennis biscuits (1½ packets)
125 g butter/margarine
5 ml ground ginger (1 t)

FILLING
15 ml gelatine (1 T)
60 ml water (¼ c)
1 tin (380 g) caramel condensed milk
15 ml smooth apricot jam (1 T)
75 ml finely chopped ginger preserve (5 T)
1 tin (410 g) well-chilled evaporated milk
125 ml cream (½ c)

Crumble the Marie or Tennis biscuits. Melt the butter/margarine and stir with the ginger into the biscuit crumbs. Reserve a little of the crumb mixture to sprinkle over the filling later. Firmly press the remaining crumbs with the back of a metal spoon onto the sides and base of two pie dishes, each having a volume of approximately 750 ml (3 c).

Soak the gelatine in the water and then clarify it over boiling water. Mix the soaked gelatine well with the caramel condensed milk, apricot jam and 50 ml (3 T) of the ginger preserve.

Beat the evaporated milk until it is thick and frothy. Fold the beaten evaporated milk into the preserve mixture. Pour the filling into the crusts and chill till set.

Beat the cream until it is stiff. Decorate the tarts with the whipped cream, the remaining 30 ml (2 T) of the ginger preserve and the reserved crumb mixture.

Makes 2 medium tarts

CAKES

It is most satisfying to bake a cake, whether it be a fruit cake, a layer cake or simply a hot teacake. In order to ensure success, it is most important to follow the recipe exactly. Don't give in to the temptation to double the ingredients and to bake two cakes in the time it takes to bake one. Instead of one excellent cake, all you'll end up with is two cakes which are not quite up to standard, or worse still – two flops.

BUTTERMILK CHOCOLATE CAKE

You can never have enough chocolate cake, as long as it is moist and dark. With this recipe from my mother's cookbook, you can make a proper cake – big enough for family and visitors. If you don't have buttermilk on hand, replace it with the same amount of fresh milk combined with the juice of half a lemon.

BATTER
80 g cocoa (1 c)
200 ml boiling water (¾ c)
500 g castor sugar (2½ c)
230 g butter/margarine (1 c)
5 extra large eggs
400 g cake flour (3 c)
5 ml baking powder (1 t)
1 ml salt (¼ t)
375 ml buttermilk (1½ c)
5 ml bicarbonate of soda (1 t)
5 ml vanilla essence (1 t)

ICING
60 ml cocoa (4 T)
5 ml instant coffee powder (1 t)
50 g butter/margarine (4 T)
1 tin (397 g) condensed milk
5 ml vanilla essence (1 t)
500 g icing sugar (3¾ c)

Sift the cocoa and mix to a paste with the boiling water. Leave to cool.

Preheat the oven to 180 °C. Grease three 22 cm layer cake pans and cover the base of each pan with waxed paper.

Cream the castor sugar and butter/margarine. Add the eggs one at a time, beating well. After every 2 eggs add a tablespoon of cake flour. Stir in the cocoa.

Sift the remaining cake flour, baking powder and salt. Mix the buttermilk, bicarbonate of soda and vanilla essence. Stir the flour and buttermilk mixtures alternately into the egg mixture, beginning and ending with the flour mixture.

Spoon an equal quantity of batter into each pan and spread evenly. Bake for about 35 minutes until done. Leave to cool in the pans for a few minutes. Loosen the sides, if necessary, and invert the layers onto wire racks. Remove the paper and leave the cake layers to cool.

Sift together the cocoa and coffee powder. Add the butter/margarine and heat till melted. Stir until there are no lumps.

Mix the cocoa mixture, condensed milk and vanilla essence. Sift the icing sugar over this and mix to a smooth icing.

Fill and ice the cake. Chill it overnight before cutting.

Makes a large three-layer cake

CAKES 97

COCONUT LAYER CAKE

My family loves everything containing coconut and this coconut layer cake is an old family favourite. It consists of soft cake layers covered with a delectable cooked coconut filling. Leave the filling to cool completely before using.

BATTER
125 g butter/margarine
200 g castor sugar (1 c)
3 extra large eggs
275 g cake flour (2 c)
12,5 ml baking powder (2½ t)
1 ml salt (¼ t)
150 ml milk (⅔ c)
15 ml finely grated orange rind (1 T)

FILLING
250 g coconut (2½ c)
200 g sugar (1 c)
125 ml milk (½ c)
125 ml water (½ c)
3 egg yolks

Preheat the oven to 190 °C. Grease two layer cake pans with a diameter of 20 cm. Line the bases with waxed paper.

Cream the butter/margarine and castor sugar. Add the eggs one at a time and beat well after each addition.

Sift together the cake flour, baking powder and salt. Stir the flour mixture and the milk alternately into the egg mixture. Stir in the orange rind.

Spoon an equal amount of batter into each pan and spread evenly. Bake the cake layers for about 35 minutes until done. Leave to cool in the pans for a few minutes. Carefully loosen the sides, if necessary, and invert the cake layers onto wire racks. Carefully remove the waxed paper and leave the cake layers to cool.

Mix the filling ingredients in a small saucepan. Slowly bring to the boil and stir continuously. Leave to cool. Spread half the filling onto each cake layer and place the layers of cake on top of each other.

Makes a medium two-layer cake

ORANGE LAYER CAKE

Because I grew up in Rustenburg, I can never forget the fragrance of orange blossoms or the orchards full of oranges. With an orange orchard in our back yard, we baked orange cake quite often.

BATTER
250 g castor sugar (1¼ c)
125 g butter/margarine
4 extra large eggs
5 ml finely grated orange rind (1 t)
200 g cake flour (1½ c)
70 g cornflour (½ c)
10 ml baking powder (2 t)
1 ml salt (¼ t)
125 ml orange juice (½ c)

ICING
125 g butter/margarine
400 g icing sugar (3 c)
50 ml granadilla pulp (3 T)
1 egg yolk
15 ml finely grated orange rind (1 T)

Preheat the oven to 180 °C. Grease two 20 cm layer cake pans. Line the bases of the pans with waxed paper.

Cream the castor sugar and the butter/margarine. Separate the eggs. Beat the egg yolks one at a time into the sugar mixture. Stir in the orange rind.

Sift together the cake flour, cornflour, baking powder and salt. Stir the flour mixture and the orange juice alternately into the sugar mixture. Beat the egg whites till soft peaks form. Fold into the batter. Spoon the batter into the pans and spread evenly. Bake the cake layers for approximately 40 minutes till done. Leave to cool in the pans for a while before carefully turning out onto a wire rack and removing the paper.

Beat the butter/margarine and 130 g (1 c) of the icing sugar till light. Beat in the remaining icing sugar, the granadilla pulp, egg yolk and orange rind. Fill and ice the cake layers with the icing.

Makes a medium two-layer cake

JONKERSHOEK CHEESECAKE

There was a tea garden in the Jonkershoek valley which served a cheesecake like this.

CRUST
125 g butter/margarine
30 ml castor sugar (2 T)
15 ml sunflower oil (1 T)
1 extra large egg
275 g cake flour (2 c)
10 ml baking powder (2 t)
pinch of salt

FILLING
4 extra large eggs
200 g sugar (1 c)
50 ml lemon juice (3 T)
15 ml finely grated lemon rind (1 T)
3 containers (250 g each) smooth cottage cheese
250 ml cream (1 c)
50 g cake flour (5½ T)
2 ml salt (½ t)

Grease a loose-bottomed cake pan, 22 cm in diameter and 7,5 cm deep, and line the base and sides with waxed paper. Preheat the oven to 160 °C.

Cream the butter/margarine, castor sugar, sunflower oil and egg. Sift together the cake flour, baking powder and salt. Combine the flour mixture thoroughly with the creamed mixture. Press three-quarters of the dough against the sides and base of the pan and crimp the edge. Chill the crust and the scraps of dough.

Beat the eggs and sugar until lemon in colour and thick and spongy. Add the remaining filling ingredients and beat to combine. Pour the filling into the crust. Roughly grate the scraps of dough on top.

Bake the cake for 1¼ hours. Switch off the oven, open the oven door slightly and leave the cake in the oven to cool.

Remove the cheesecake very carefully from the cake pan and remove the paper without breaking the crust.

Makes a large cheesecake

ALMOND CAKE

All the men in our family just love this almond cake because it is full of flavour, but it isn't really very sweet. Even my stepson, Hannto, who has no liking for sweet things, eats a second slice of this cake whenever I make it.

150 g castor sugar (¾ c)
125 g butter/margarine
275 g cake flour (2 c)
15 ml baking powder (1 T)
1 ml salt (¼ t)
3 extra large eggs
60 ml milk (¼ c)
60 ml water (¼ c)
1 ml almond essence (¼ t)
50 ml finely chopped almonds (3 T)
30 ml soft brown sugar (2 T)
7 ml cinnamon (1½ t)

Grease a deep cake pan with a diameter of approximately 22 cm and line the base of the pan with waxed paper.

Cream the castor sugar with the butter/margarine. Sift together the cake flour, baking powder and salt. Beat the eggs one at a time into the sugar mixture and after each addition add a tablespoon of the flour mixture.

Mix together the milk, the water and the almond essence. Stir the milk mixture and the remaining flour mixture alternately into the sugar mixture.

Spoon the batter into the pan and spread evenly. Mix the almonds, brown sugar and cinnamon. Sprinkle on top.

Place the cake in a cold oven. Heat the oven to 160 °C. Bake the cake for about 30–35 minutes after the oven temperature has reached 160 °C.

Carefully remove the cake from the pan and peel off the waxed paper. Leave the cake to cool before serving.

Makes a medium cake

HOT TEACAKE

During my childhood, whenever we nagged my mother for a piece of hot, just-baked cake, she always warned us that we'd get a terrible tummyache if we ate hot cake. When I came across this recipe one fine day, everyone in the family was delighted, because at last we were allowed to eat hot cake.

BATTER
140 g cake flour (1 c)
5 ml baking powder (1 t)
1 ml salt (¼ t)
150 g sugar (¾ c)
2 extra large eggs
5 ml vanilla essence (1 t)
125 ml milk (½ c)
30 ml butter/margarine (2 T)

SYRUP
60 ml water (¼ c)
50 g butter/margarine (4 T)
30 ml golden syrup (2 T)

Preheat the oven to 190 °C. Grease a shallow, ovenproof dish with a volume of about 1,5 litres (6 c).

Sift together the cake flour, baking powder and salt. Beat together the sugar, eggs and vanilla essence until lemon in colour and thick and spongy. Heat the milk and the butter/margarine until lukewarm and stir the milk mixture until the butter/margarine has melted.

Lightly fold the flour mixture into the egg mixture with a metal spoon. Add the milk mixture and fold in lightly. Pour the batter into the dish.

Bake the cake for about 30 minutes till done and light brown on top.

Bring the water, butter/margarine and golden syrup to the boil. Pour this mixture over the hot cake just after it has been taken from the oven. Leave the cake to cool until lukewarm and serve in the dish.

Makes a medium cake

SWISS ROLL

Sometimes I replace the apricot jam in this recipe with strawberry jam. Using this variation, I can serve slices of the Swiss roll as a delicious dessert heaped with fresh strawberries and cream.

   3 extra large eggs
   200 g sugar (1 c)
   30 ml sunflower oil (2 T)
   5 ml vanilla essence (1 t)
   140 g cake flour (1 c)
   10 ml baking powder (2 t)
   1 ml salt (¼ t)
   60 ml milk (¼ c)
   200 ml smooth apricot jam (¾ c)

Preheat the oven to 200 °C. Grease a Swiss roll tin, 40 cm x 27 cm x 2 cm, and line it with waxed paper.

Beat together the eggs and 150 g (⅔ c) of the sugar till lemon in colour and thick and spongy. Beat the sunflower oil and vanilla essence into the sugar mixture.

Sift the cake flour, baking powder and salt. Stir the flour mixture and the milk alternately into the egg mixture. Spread the batter in the tin. Bake the Swiss roll for about 10 minutes until golden brown.

Sprinkle the remaining 50 g (4 T) of sugar onto a damp cloth. Turn out the hot Swiss roll onto it and carefully peel off the waxed paper. Trim the edges neatly. Roll up the cake with the cloth.

Warm the apricot jam slightly. Open out the Swiss roll and spread with jam. Roll up again, but without the cloth. Place on a wire rack to cool.

Makes a medium Swiss roll

FILLING A SWISS ROLL WITH CREAM

Leave the Swiss roll, while it is rolled up in the damp cloth, to cool completely. Then unroll it carefully, spread with jam and stiffly beaten cream, and roll it up, but without the cloth.

NUT AND SULTANA RING CAKE

If you don't have the time to make a traditional dark fruitcake for Christmas, this fruitcake is the ideal alternative.

    100 g mixed nuts (1 c)
    250 g butter/margarine
    200 g castor sugar (1 c)
    275 g cake flour (2 c)
    2 ml baking powder (½ t)
    2 ml salt (½ t)
    4 extra large eggs
    150 g sultanas (1 c)
    150 g mixed candied peel (1 c)
    15 ml finely grated lemon rind (1 T)
    50 ml lemon juice (3 T)
    50 ml brandy (3 T)

    ICING
    100 g icing sugar (¾ c)
    15 ml water (1 T)
    5 ml lemon juice (1 t)
    few chopped nuts

Preheat the oven to 180 °C. Grease a ring pan with a diameter of approximately 22 cm. Line the pan with waxed paper. Chop the nuts fairly finely.

Cream the butter/margarine and castor sugar. Sift together the cake flour, baking powder and salt. Beat the eggs one at a time into the sugar mixture together with a tablespoon of the flour mixture.

Mix the nuts, sultanas and candied peel with the remaining flour mixture. Add to the sugar mixture and stir till blended. Stir in the lemon rind and juice.

Spoon the batter into the pan and spread evenly. Bake for about 30 minutes. Lower the oven temperature to 160 °C and bake for another 40 minutes.

Turn the cake out onto a wire cooling rack. Peel off the paper and sprinkle the cake with the brandy. Leave it to cool.

Mix the icing sugar, water and lemon juice to a paste and trickle it over the cake. Sprinkle with nuts immediately.

Makes a medium ring cake

SHORT AND SWEET FRUIT CAKE

This cake has few ingredients, is moist and full of fruit – perfect for Christmas.

    100 g glacé cherries (22 whole)
    1,35 kg dried fruit cake mix (9 c)
    250 ml rum/brandy (1 c)
    250 g soft brown sugar (1¼ c)
    230 g butter/margarine (1 c)
    5 extra large eggs
    240 g cake flour (1¾ c)
    125 ml honey (½ c)
    2 ml bicarbonate of soda (½ t)

Halve the glacé cherries. Add the dried fruit cake mix and rum/brandy and mix. Cover and leave to stand for a few hours.

Grease a deep 25 cm cake pan. Line the base and sides with a double layer of waxed paper and grease the paper too. Tie a double layer of brown paper on the outside of the pan. Also fold a 'lid' from a double layer of brown paper.

Preheat the oven to 160 °C. Cream the brown sugar and butter/margarine. Separate the eggs. Beat the egg yolks one by one into the sugar mixture, and after each addition stir in a tablespoon of the flour. Beat the mixture well each time. Mix the remaining flour with the fruit mixture and stir into the sugar mixture.

Heat the honey, mix it with the bicarbonate of soda and stir it into the fruit mixture. Beat the egg whites till they form stiff peaks and fold into the fruit mixture.

Spoon the batter into the pan. Place the 'lid' on top. Bake the cake for 90 minutes. Lower the oven temperature to 140 °C and bake it for another hour. (If a skewer inserted into the middle of the cake comes out clean, the cake is done.)

Sprinkle the hot cake with a little extra rum/brandy and leave to cool in the pan. Carefully turn it out and store it in an airtight container till needed. Remove the waxed paper just before cutting.

Makes a large fruit cake

SMALL CAKES AND BISCUITS

When you have a tinful of small cakes and biscuits in the house, you're always ready for guests or children who want something to nibble. If you also keep koeksisters in the freezer, no-one can catch you unprepared. Baking biscuits can become a social event if mother and daughter or two friends get together to set about filling the cake tins. Many hands not only make light work, but also plenty of cakes and biscuits in a short time.

KOEKSISTERS

Women judge a koeksister by its crispness and the amount of syrup that runs out of it. Men, however, complain if there's too much syrup – it's too sweet, they say, and it drips on one's shoes. These koeksisters are full of syrup that stays inside.

SYRUP
3 pieces of whole ginger
1,2 kg sugar (6 c)
750 ml water (3 c)
15 ml golden syrup (1 T)
5 ml lemon juice (1 t)
2 ml cream of tartar (½ t)

DOUGH
540 g cake flour (4 c)
30 ml baking powder (2 T)
5 ml ground nutmeg (1 t)
2 ml salt (½ t)
50 g butter/margarine (4 T)
375 ml milk (1½ c)
sunflower oil

Bruise the ginger and tie it in a cloth. Bring the sugar, water, golden syrup, lemon juice, cream of tartar and ginger to the boil in an open saucepan, stirring occasionally, but only while the syrup has not yet boiled. Put on the lid when the syrup begins to boil and boil for a minute. Remove the lid, reduce the temperature of the stove and boil the syrup for a further 5 minutes. Chill overnight.

Sift together the cake flour, baking powder, nutmeg and salt. Rub in the butter/margarine. Cut in the milk with a spatula until it forms a stiff dough. Knead lightly. Cover the dough and leave it to rest for at least an hour.

Grease a pastry board and rolling pin with a little oil. Roll out the dough to a thickness of 7 mm. Cut the dough into strips, 20 cm x 1 cm. Shape koeksisters from the strips. Keep the strips and koeksisters covered with a damp cloth.

Pour the syrup into a deep dish inside a larger dish with iced water and ice cubes.

Pour sunflower oil to a depth of 5 cm into a saucepan with a diameter of 20 cm. Heat over moderate heat till hot. (A bit of raw dough should rise to the surface after a count of 10.) Place the koeksisters a few at a time into the hot oil. Fry one side till golden brown and then the other side.

Immediately plunge the cooked koeksisters into the ice cold syrup. Hold under the syrup for a count of 5, remove with a slotted spoon and set on a wire rack in a tray. Chill or freeze the koeksisters.

Makes about 7 dozen koeksisters

SMALL CAKES AND BISCUITS 107

QUICK DOUGHNUTS

These doughnuts are light in texture and easy to make. Handle the dough as little as possible and cut out the circles very close together so that there is little dough left over to be rolled out again. I either ice the doughnuts with a little glacé icing or I dust them with castor sugar. They freeze well.

   250 ml buttermilk (1 c)
   200 g sugar (1 c)
   2 extra large eggs
   50 g butter/margarine (4 T)
   600 g cake flour (4½ c)
   20 ml baking powder (4 t)
   5 ml ground nutmeg (1 t)
   2 ml salt (½ t)
   1 ml bicarbonate of soda (¼ t)
   sunflower oil
   castor sugar

Beat together the buttermilk, sugar and eggs. Melt the butter/margarine and beat into the buttermilk mixture.

Sift together the cake flour, baking powder, nutmeg, salt and bicarbonate of soda. Using a spatula, cut the buttermilk mixture into the flour mixture till blended.

Grease a pastry board and rolling pin with a little oil. Roll out the dough to a thickness of about 1 cm. Cut out circles measuring 7,5 cm in diameter. Cut out a smaller circle, 2,5 cm in diameter, from the middle of each to make a hole.

Pour sunflower oil to a depth of 5 cm into a medium saucepan. Heat the oil till moderately hot. Place the rings and little balls into the oil, a few at a time. First fry them on one side until golden brown and then on the other side.

Drain the cooked doughnuts on paper towelling. Sprinkle each one with a little castor sugar while still hot and serve.

Makes 15 rings and 48 little balls

AUNT CLASINA'S CUP CAKES

As a young schoolgirl in 1938, my mother stayed with aunt Clasina Kruger in Rustenburg. Aunt Clasina often baked these old-fashioned teacakes for them. She sometimes added coconut or currants.

BATTER
230 g butter/margarine (1 c)
200 g castor sugar (1 c)
4 extra large eggs
540 g cake flour (4 c)
20 ml baking powder (4 t)
1 ml salt (¼ t)
300 ml milk (1¼ c)
5 ml vanilla essence (1 t)

ICING
400 g icing sugar (3 c)
50 ml milk (3 T)
25 ml melted butter/margarine (5 t)
25 ml lemon juice (5 t)
hundreds-and-thousands

Preheat the oven to 190 °C. Put paper cases into the hollows of patty pans.

Cream the butter/margarine and the castor sugar. Add the eggs one at a time, beating very well after each addition. Sift together the cake flour, baking powder and salt. Mix the milk and vanilla essence. Stir the flour mixture and the milk mixture alternately and a little at a time into the egg mixture, beginning and ending with the flour mixture, to form a batter.

Fill the paper cases three-quarters full of batter. Bake the cup cakes for 15 minutes until they start to brown. Leave to cool.

Sift the icing sugar. Add the remaining ingredients, except the hundreds-and-thousands, and beat to make a smooth icing. Spread the icing on the cup cakes and immediately scatter a few hundreds-and-thousands on top.

Makes 56 cup cakes

FRUIT SQUARES

If you have to come up with an attractive plate of eats in a hurry, these splendid little fridge bars would be a good choice. They are made of Tennis biscuits covered with a heavenly fruit mixture which not only looks good, but tastes wonderful.

    2 packets (200 g each) Tennis biscuits
    500 g dried fruit cake mix (3 c)
    230 g butter/margarine (1 c)
    100 g sugar (½ c)
    100 g chopped glacé cherries (½ c)
    2 extra large eggs
    15 ml finely grated lemon rind (1 T)
    30 ml toasted coconut (2 T)

Cover the base of a Swiss roll tin measuring about 33 cm x 23 cm, with some of the Tennis biscuits. Lay the biscuits upside down in the tin and trim them with a serrated knife where necessary for them to fit in. Crumble the remaining biscuits roughly and set them aside.

Bring the dried fruit cake mix, butter/margarine, sugar and glacé cherries to the boil over moderate heat, stirring at regular intervals. Beat the eggs. Mix the beaten eggs very quickly with the boiling fruit mixture. (If you do not mix very quickly, the liquid of the fruit mixture becomes lumpy, because the egg sets before the whole amount has been stirred in.) Stir the mixture over low heat until it thickens. Add the lemon rind and reserved biscuit crumbs and mix well.

Spread the fruit mixture over the layer of biscuits in the tin and press it down well. Sprinkle the coconut on top of the fruit mixture. Chill it until firm. Cut into squares, 4 cm x 4 cm.

Makes 4 dozen squares

FRECKLES

Instead of using the handle of a wooden spoon to make hollows in the dough, you can use a thimble. The bigger the hollow, the prettier the biscuit, but beware of putting in too much jam, as it can easily bubble out during the baking process and spoil the look of the biscuits.

> 90 g cornflakes (3 c)
> 300 g cake flour (2¼ c)
> 100 g sugar (½ c)
> 1 ml salt (¼ t)
> 230 g butter/margarine (1 c)
> 5 ml finely grated lemon rind (1 t)
> 2 extra large eggs
> 60 ml smooth apricot jam (¼ c)
> red food colouring

Preheat the oven to 180 °C.

Crush the cornflakes finely with a rolling pin. Mix the cake flour, the sugar and the salt. Add half of the cornflake crumbs to the flour mixture and combine well. Rub the butter/margarine and the lemon rind into the flour mixture. Beat the eggs. Mix the beaten eggs well with the flour mixture to form a soft dough.

Roll little balls from the dough, each using 10 ml (2 t) of the dough. Roll each ball in the remaining cornflake crumbs. Place them a little apart on baking sheets and flatten slightly with a fork. Press a hollow in the middle of each flattened ball with the handle of a wooden spoon.

Colour the apricot jam with a drop or two of the red food colouring. Spoon a little apricot jam into each hollow.

Bake the biscuits for about 15 minutes until they start to brown.

Makes 56 biscuits

GINGER BISCUITS

About 30 years ago, I cut out this recipe from a newspaper and pasted it in my recipe book. I've always wanted to make these biscuits, but somehow I never got round to it. What a loss, because they are marvellous biscuits – flat, crisp, full of cracks and particularly tasty.

- 450 g sugar (2¼ c)
- 350 g butter/margarine (1½ c)
- 2 extra large eggs
- 75 ml golden syrup (⅓ c)
- 475 g cake flour (3½ c)
- 10 ml bicarbonate of soda (2 t)
- 10 ml cinnamon (2 t)
- 10 ml ground ginger (2 t)
- 5 ml ground cloves (1 t)
- 2 ml salt (½ t)

Preheat the oven to 180 °C. Grease two or three baking sheets. Cream 350 g (1¾ c) of the sugar with the butter/margarine. Beat in the eggs one at a time. Stir in the golden syrup. Sift together the cake flour, bicarbonate of soda, cinnamon, ginger, cloves and salt. Combine the flour mixture well with the sugar mixture to form a soft dough. Chill the dough for a while.

Roll pieces of dough between your palms to make little balls, each 2,5 cm in diameter. Roll the balls in the remaining sugar and place on the greased baking sheets about 5 cm apart.

Bake the biscuits for about 12 minutes till nice and brown. Cool the biscuits on the baking sheets until quite hard before removing with an egg slice and placing on wire racks to cool completely.

Store the biscuits in an airtight container so that their flavour can develop fully and so that they remain crisp, because they quickly become soft if they are left open.

Makes 9½ dozen biscuits

DATE BARS

This is my version of a very old recipe from Mrs Slade's cookbook Cakes and Puddings. *These date bars are delightful.*

   500 g stoned dates
   250 ml water (1 c)
   60 ml orange juice (¼ c)
   5 ml finely grated orange rind (1 t)
   225 g sugar (1 c and 2 T)
   400 g cake flour (3 c)
   5 ml cinnamon (1 t)
   2 ml salt (½ t)
   2 ml bicarbonate of soda (½ t)
   175 g butter/margarine (¾ c)
   150 g oats (1½ c)
   125 ml milk (½ c)
   2 extra large eggs

Preheat the oven to 190 °C. Grease a square cake pan, 24 cm x 24 cm. Line the base with waxed paper.

Cut the dates into pieces. Add the water, orange juice and rind and 100 g (½ c) of the sugar. Cook slowly to a pulp and stir at regular intervals. Leave to cool.

Sift together the cake flour, cinnamon, salt, bicarbonate of soda and 100 g (½ c) of the remaining sugar. Rub in the butter/margarine. Add the oats to the flour mixture and mix. Beat the milk with one of the eggs. Mix the milk mixture with the flour mixture to form a soft dough.

Press half the dough into the cake pan. Spread the filling over the dough. On a piece of waxed paper roll the remaining dough to the same size. Invert it over the filling and carefully peel off the paper.

Beat the remaining egg and brush the dough with it. Sprinkle the remaining 25 g (2 T) sugar over the dough.

Bake the pastry for about 45 minutes till light brown. Leave to cool in the pan for a while. Invert carefully onto a wire rack to cool completely. Remove the paper and cut the pastry into 6 cm x 3 cm bars.

Makes 32 bars

114 SMALL CAKES AND BISCUITS

LEMON CREAMS

Biscuits with fillings are always more popular than plain biscuits. When they are melt-in-the-mouth lemon creams with their lemony taste and soft filling to boot, the plate is empty in a flash.

DOUGH
700 g butter/margarine (3 c)
600 g sugar (3 c)
4 extra large eggs
50 ml milk (3 T)
50 ml finely grated lemon rind (3 T)
1,5 kg cake flour (11 c)
50 g baking powder (3½ T)
10 ml cream of tartar (2 t)
5 ml salt (1 t)
1 egg white

FILLING
500 g icing sugar
250 g butter/margarine
1 egg yolk
15 ml finely grated lemon rind (1 T)
5 ml lemon essence (1 t)
5 ml glycerine (1 t)
2 ml citric acid (½ t)

Cream together the butter/margarine and sugar. Beat in the eggs one at a time. Stir in the milk and lemon rind.

Sift together the cake flour, baking powder, cream of tartar and salt. Add the egg mixture and mix very well.

Preheat the oven to 190 °C. Grease baking sheets. Roll the dough to a thickness of about 5 mm on a floured pastry board. Cut out circles or shapes with a diameter of approximately 5 cm. Place them slightly apart on the baking sheets. Beat the egg white slightly. Lightly brush each biscuit with the beaten egg white and sprinkle with a little extra sugar.

Bake the biscuits for about 10 minutes until they begin to brown. Leave to cool on a wire rack before filling them.

Sift the icing sugar well. Add the butter/margarine and beat until well combined. Add the remaining filling ingredients and mix very well.

Sandwich two biscuits at a time, using the filling generously.

Makes about 14 dozen filled biscuits

CUSTARD BISCUITS

These biscuits are made with a cookie gun or with a biscuit maker attached to a mincer. Don't grease the baking sheets if using a cookie gun.

400 g cake flour (3 c)
130 g custard powder (1 c)
20 ml baking powder (4 t)
1 ml salt (¼ t)
250 g butter/margarine
200 g sugar (1 c)
2 extra large eggs
5 ml vanilla essence (1 t)
30 glacé cherries

Preheat the oven to 180 °C.

Sift together the cake flour, custard powder, baking powder and salt. Cream together the butter/margarine, sugar, eggs and vanilla essence. Gradually add the flour mixture to the creamed mixture and combine well to form a soft dough.

Shape the dough into biscuits with a cookie gun or a biscuit maker. Place them slightly apart on baking sheets. Quarter the glacé cherries and decorate each biscuit with a piece of cherry.

Bake the biscuits for about 12 minutes until they begin to turn brown. Lift the hot biscuits very carefully from the baking sheets with an egg slice and leave them to cool completely on a wire rack.

Makes about 10 dozen biscuits

JAM SLICES

Jam slices are evergreen favourites and you can never get bored with them, no matter how often they are baked. Although apricot jam is my family's personal favourite, other kinds of jam are also suitable for these slices.

230 g butter/margarine (1 c)
200 g sugar (1 c)
2 extra large eggs
10 ml vanilla essence (2 t)
540 g cake flour (4 c)
15 ml baking powder (1 T)
2 ml salt (½ t)
375 ml smooth apricot jam (1½ c)
60 g coconut (¾ c)
130 g icing sugar (1 c)
20–25 ml lemon juice (4–5 t)

Preheat the oven to 190 °C. Lightly grease a baking tray, 45 cm x 30 cm x 2,5 cm. Cream together the butter/margarine and sugar. Beat in the eggs one at a time. Add the vanilla essence and mix. Sift together the cake flour, baking powder and salt. Add the flour mixture to the egg mixture and combine to form a dough.

Press two-thirds of the dough into the baking tray. Spread apricot jam over the dough and sprinkle the coconut on top. Grate the remaining dough on top.

Bake the pastry for 20–25 minutes until it starts to brown on top. First trim the edges of the hot pastry and then cut it into rectangles, 6 cm x 3,5 cm. Leave the rectangles to cool on a wire rack.

Mix the icing sugar with just enough of the lemon juice to form a dropping consistency. Trickle the icing over the slices and leave them to dry.

Makes 56 slices

SIELIE'S SPICE BISCUITS

Cecilia Wentzel of Witrand, between Koster and Zwartruggens, was a formidable lady. Aunt Sielie, as I remember her from my youth, was big, strict and wore a bun, but she always served these magnificent spice biscuits with coffee or ginger beer to children or visitors. When ma Judith, her daughter and now my mother-in-law, visits us, she always bakes Sielie's spice biscuits for us. The lard makes them beautifully crisp.

1,25 kg cake flour (9 c)
50 g baking powder (3½ T)
15 ml cinnamon (1 T)
7 ml salt (1½ t)
2 ml ground cloves (½ t)
250 g butter/margarine
250 g lard
5 extra large eggs
600 g sugar (3 c)
1 egg yolk
30 ml milk (2 T)

Preheat the oven to 190 °C. Grease two or three baking sheets.

Sift together the cake flour, baking powder, cinnamon, salt and cloves. Rub in the butter/margarine and lard till well mixed. Beat the eggs with the sugar until thick and creamy. Add the egg mixture to the flour mixture and combine well to form quite a firm dough.

Roll out the dough to a thickness of about 5 mm. (Flour the rolling pin lightly if the dough tends to stick to it.) Cut out circles or shapes, about 6 cm in diameter. Place the circles or shapes close together on the baking sheets.

Beat the egg yolk with the milk. Brush the biscuits with this mixture.

Bake the biscuits for about 12 minutes until they are slightly brown. Place the biscuits on a wire rack to cool. Store them in an airtight container.

Makes approximately 18 dozen biscuits

SMALL CAKES AND BISCUITS

CRUNCHIES

In a home full of warmth, children's voices and the hurly-burly of everyday living, there should always be a tinful of these wonderful coarse coconut biscuits.

Crunchies are usually cut into squares after baking, but I prefer to roll the raw dough into little balls.

    400 g sugar (2 c)
    275 g cake flour (2 c)
    200 g oats (2 c)
    160 g coconut (2 c)
    5 ml salt (1 t)
    230 g butter/margarine (1 c)
    50 ml water (3 T)
    30 ml golden syrup (2 T)
    10 ml bicarbonate of soda (2 t)
    1 extra large egg
    10 ml vanilla essence (2 t)

Mix the sugar, cake flour, oats, coconut and salt. Heat the butter/margarine, water and golden syrup until the shortening has melted. Add the bicarbonate of soda (it froths a lot) and mix the butter/margarine mixture with the flour mixture. Beat the egg with the vanilla essence. Add this to the flour mixture and mix well to form a soft dough. Cover the dough and chill until it is more manageable.

Preheat the oven to 190 °C. Roll pieces of dough between the palms to make little balls. Place slightly apart on baking sheets and flatten each ball with a fork.

Bake the biscuits for about 8 minutes until golden brown. Leave them to cool slightly on the baking sheets before lifting onto a wire rack with an egg slice. Leave to cool completely. Store the biscuits in an airtight container.

Makes about 9 dozen biscuits

JACOBA'S CRISPY BISCUITS

The name Jacoba Willemse will remind many an ex-Matie of her hospitality and the big, friendly old house in Stellenbosch where they were always so at home. Jacoba was a hard-working, gentle lady who loved to write poetry. After her death, her children published her poems in the little volume Verse van Jacoba.

Jacoba could also cook and bake wonderfully. One of my favourites are her crispy, crunchy, puffed rice biscuits.

400 g sugar (2 c)
350 g butter/margarine (1½ c)
2 extra large eggs
5 ml vanilla essence (1 t)
350 g cake flour (2½ c)
10 ml baking powder (2 t)
7 ml bicarbonate of soda (1½ t)
5 ml salt (1 t)
200 g oats (2 c)
160 g coconut (2 c)
60 g Rice Krispies puffed rice (2 c)

Preheat the oven to 180 °C.

Cream the sugar, butter/margarine and eggs. Sift together the cake flour, baking powder, bicarbonate of soda and salt. Add the oats and the coconut to the flour mixture and mix thoroughly. Add the puffed rice and mix lightly.

Roll pieces of dough between the palms to form little balls. Place them slightly apart on baking sheets.

Bake the biscuits for about 8 minutes until they are golden brown.

Leave the biscuits to cool on the baking sheets for a while before lifting them onto a wire rack with an egg slice and leaving them to cool completely. Store the biscuits in an airtight container.

Makes approximately 15 dozen biscuits

ICED CHOCOLATE SHORTCAKE

When I need a plate of eats for a special occasion, I often make this shortcake. It is also good without the marshmallows. In that case, spread the chocolate icing over the hot shortcake just before cutting.

SHORTCAKE
275 g cake flour (2 c)
30 ml cocoa (2 T)
5 ml baking powder (1 t)
2 ml salt (½ t)
160 g coconut (2 c)
250 g butter/margarine
150 g sugar (¾ c)

ICING
200 g marshmallows (24 whole)
130 g icing sugar (1 c)
15 ml cocoa (1 T)
30 ml butter/margarine (2 T)
15 ml water (1 T)
5 ml vanilla essence (1 t)

Preheat the oven to 180 °C.

Sift together the cake flour, cocoa, baking powder and salt. Add the coconut and mix. Melt the butter/margarine and sugar. Add to the flour mixture and mix well. Using a fork press the mixture firmly into a baking tray, 33 cm x 23 cm x 2 cm. Bake the shortcake for about 30 minutes until done and light brown.

In the meantime, halve the marshmallows and make the icing.

Sift together the icing sugar and the cocoa. Melt the butter/margarine and add the water and vanilla essence. Stir the butter/margarine mixture into the cocoa mixture and beat to make a smooth icing.

Cut the hot shortcake immediately after removing from the oven into squares measuring about 4 cm x 4 cm. Place half a marshmallow on each square and trickle the icing on top. Leave the shortcake to cool in the baking tray until cold.

Makes 4 dozen squares

CRESCENTS

These biscuits are real conversation pieces and remind each person of something different. Here are a few of the names offered by family and friends: horseshoes, magnets, donkey-tracks ... they even remind one of our friends of cutworms, which he must obviously adore, because he eats handfuls of these biscuits whenever he has the opportunity.

    400 g sugar (2 c)
    175 g butter/margarine (¾ c)
    2 extra large eggs
    50 ml milk (3 T)
    540 g cake flour (4 c)
    15 ml baking powder (1 T)
    2 ml salt (½ t)
    2 ml ground nutmeg (½ t)
    250 g cooking chocolate

Preheat the oven to 190 °C. Lightly grease baking sheets. Cream the sugar with the butter/margarine and eggs. Stir in the milk. Sift together the cake flour, baking powder, salt and nutmeg. Add to the sugar mixture and mix well. Cover the dough and chill for a while.

Press the dough through the cheese straw aperture of a biscuit maker. Cut the dough into 9 cm lengths, bend them into the shape of horseshoes and place slightly apart on the baking sheets.

Bake the biscuits for about 10 minutes until they begin to turn brown. Cool the biscuits on a wire rack.

Break the chocolate into small pieces and melt it in a deep dish over hot water. Dip the ends of the biscuits in the melted chocolate and place the biscuits on waxed paper to dry completely.

Makes about 18 dozen biscuits

SMALL CAKES AND BISCUITS

VETKOEK, SCONES AND MUFFINS

Vetkoek, scones and muffins are everyday stand-bys that always turn up trumps, but needn't be boring because they can so easily be varied. Where would you find a more delicious mouthful than a vetkoek full of fruit with its unexpected taste of aniseed? Or what about a scone as big as the frying pan in which it was 'baked' on the stove? Cut it into wedges and serve it hot with butter and apricot jam.

DEEP-FRIED CURRY VETKOEK

These succulent vetkoek with their most economical curry filling look and taste just like vetkoek made from yeast dough, but they are in fact made from a very easy baking powder dough. The vetkoek also freeze very well.

FILLING
2 large onions
30 ml sunflower oil (2 T)
4 medium potatoes
500 g minced beef
250 ml water (1 c)
10 ml medium curry powder (2 t)
10 ml salt (2 t)
pinch of pepper

DOUGH
540 g cake flour (4 c)
20 ml baking powder (4 t)
5 ml salt (1 t)
5 ml Aromat/Fondor (1 t)
30 ml butter/margarine (2 T)
1 extra large egg
325 ml soda water (1⅓ c)
sunflower oil

Peel the onions and chop finely. Sauté the onions in the sunflower oil. Peel and dice the potatoes. Add the potatoes to the onions together with the minced beef, water, curry powder, salt and pepper. Stew till done. Mash the mixture lightly with a fork. Leave to cool.

Sift together the cake flour, baking powder, salt and Aromat/Fondor. Rub the butter/margarine into the flour mixture. Beat the egg with 250 ml (1 c) of the soda water. Combine the egg mixture with the flour mixture. Add the remaining soda water and mix to form a dough.

Lightly grease a pastry board and rolling pin with sunflower oil. Divide the dough into 15 equal pieces. Thinly roll out one piece of the dough for every vetkoek to form a circle measuring approximately 15 cm in diameter. Dampen the edge of each circle with a little cold water and place a tablespoonful of the filling in the middle of each circle. Fold the dough over the filling and press together tightly at the top and sides.

Fry the filled vetkoek in moderately hot, deep sunflower oil until golden and cooked on top. Drain the vetkoek on paper towelling and serve hot.

Makes 15 vetkoek

VETKOEK, SCONES AND MUFFINS 123

SWEETCORN VETKOEK

A couple of years ago, almost the whole of our farm went up in flames because of a devastating veld fire. For two whole days people came to the farm from near and far to help us fight the fire. My mother and I saw to it that there was always something for them all to eat and drink. Mother Martie just kept on tirelessly frying vetkoek on the stove. That recipe, in the course of time, evolved into this one.

1 tin (420 g) cream-style sweetcorn
60 ml milk (¼ c)
1 extra large egg
275 g cake flour (2 c)
10 ml baking powder (2 t)
2 ml salt (½ t)
sunflower oil

Beat together the sweetcorn, milk and egg till mixed. Sift together the cake flour, baking powder and salt. Add this to the sweetcorn mixture and mix.

Spoon dessertspoons of the batter into 3 mm-deep, fairly hot sunflower oil in a frying pan or shallow iron saucepan. Fry the vetkoek first on the one side and then on the other side until they turn golden brown. Drain the cooked vetkoek on paper towelling. Serve hot.

Makes 1½ dozen vetkoek

EXCEPTIONAL APRICOT JAM

This is very flavourful and tastes just right with vetkoek, scones and muffins.

Wash and stone 2 kg apricots. Place in a milk cloth bag in a saucepan of boiling water and heat to boiling point. Boil for precisely 5 minutes. Remove the bag from the water and drain slightly. Place the apricots in a saucepan and add 2 kg (10 c) sugar. Heat to boiling point and boil for 12 minutes, stirring often. Immediately spoon the hot jam into hot, sterilized jars.

FRUIT VETKOEK

I usually fry vetkoek in a large, shallow iron saucepan. Don't let the oil get too hot, otherwise the vetkoek will look golden brown and done, but still be raw on the inside. First fry the one side until it is done and then fry the other side. If you turn them too quickly, the batter won't have a chance to rise properly.

If you are making these vetkoek for tea, it is a good idea to sift a little icing sugar over them just before serving.

> 400 g self-raising flour (3 c)
> 100 g sugar (½ c)
> 2 ml salt (½ t)
> 150 g dried fruit cake mix (1 c)
> 10 ml aniseed (2 t)
> 375 ml water (1½ c)
> sunflower oil

Sift together the self-raising flour, sugar and salt. Add the dried fruit cake mix and aniseed and mix. Stir in the water.

Pour sunflower oil to a depth of 3 mm into a heavy-based pan and heat until moderately hot. Spoon dessertspoons of the batter into the oil. Fry the vetkoek on both sides until they are golden brown and done. Drain the cooked vetkoek on paper towelling and serve them hot.

Makes about 2 dozen vetkoek

INSTANT VETKOEK

For a cheaper version, omit the dried fruit cake mix and the aniseed from the recipe for Fruit Vetkoek.

Simply sift together the self-raising flour, sugar and salt and stir in the water. Fry the vetkoek in shallow sunflower oil as described in the recipe for Fruit Vetkoek.

For an even simpler vetkoek, one may even omit the sugar. The vetkoek can then be made from only the self-raising flour, salt and water.

POTATO GRIDDLE SCONES

A lovely way to have breakfast outside is to heat a large griddle over the coals and let everyone cook their own food. These griddle scones are excellent with fried bacon, eggs and halved tomatoes.

> 2 medium potatoes
> 140 g cake flour (1 c)
> 15 ml baking powder (1 T)
> 5 ml salt (1 t)
> pinch of cayenne pepper
> 50 g butter/margarine (4 T)
> 125 ml milk (½ c)

Boil the potatoes in their jackets in plenty of water until they are done. Drain and remove the skins. Press the potatoes through a sieve and leave to cool.

Heat a griddle over moderate heat. Sift together the cake flour, baking powder, salt and cayenne pepper. Rub the butter/margarine into the flour mixture until it resembles coarse mealie meal.

Add the milk to the mashed potatoes. Using a spatula, cut the potato mixture into the flour mixture. Press it together so that it forms a dough.

Place the dough on a floured pastry board. Roll it out lightly to a thickness of approximately 1 cm. Cut the dough into squares, about 7 cm x 5 cm.

Dust the griddle with a little cake flour. (If the cake flour browns immediately, the griddle has become too hot.) Place the griddle scones on it and fry them first on the one side and then on the other until they are brown and done.

Eat the scones lukewarm, halved and smothered in butter.

Makes 1 dozen griddle scones

FRYING PAN SCONE

Remember to take this recipe with you when you go on holiday to a place where you don't have an oven at your disposal. You simply 'bake' this large scone in a frying pan on the stove, or even a little to one side on the coals, then cut it into wedges and eat it with gusto.

15 ml butter/margarine (1 T)
140 g cake flour (1 c)
10 ml baking powder (2 t)
2 ml salt (½ t)
125 ml lukewarm milk (½ c)
1 extra large egg

Melt the butter/margarine over low heat in a heavy-based frying pan with a diameter of approximately 22 cm.

Sift together the cake flour, the baking powder and the salt. Beat together the milk, egg and melted butter/margarine. Cut the milk mixture into the flour mixture with a spatula till just combined.

Spoon the batter into the frying pan and spread it evenly, without handling it too much. Cover the pan.

'Bake' the scone slowly over low heat until the top feels firm when lightly pressed with a finger and the bottom has turned golden brown. Carefully turn over the scone with an egg slice. Continue to 'bake' it over low heat until the light side is also golden brown. Turn the scone out of the frying pan.

To serve, cut the hot scone into wedges, then cut open the wedges and spread lavishly with butter/margarine and golden syrup, honey or jam. The wedges of scone taste best if eaten lukewarm.

Makes 4–6 servings

ORANGE SCONES

These scones are tasty, quick to make and just the thing for breakfast. We eat them with cheese, golden syrup or honey.

260 g wholewheat flour (2 c)
30 ml soft brown sugar (2 T)
15 ml baking powder (1 T)
2 ml salt (½ t)
finely grated rind of 1 orange
125 ml orange juice (½ c)
75 ml sunflower oil (5 T)
1 extra large egg
75 g sultanas (½ c)
bran
15 ml milk (1 T)

Preheat the oven to 200 °C.

Mix the wholewheat flour, brown sugar, baking powder, salt and orange rind. Beat the orange juice with the sunflower oil and the egg. Cut the liquid into the flour mixture with a spatula to form a dough. Add the sultanas and cut in till mixed.

Sprinkle a little bran on a baking sheet. Lightly shape the dough into a ball, place the ball on the bran and press it into a 2 cm-thick circle. Cut the circle into eighths with a sharp knife. Brush the dough with the milk.

Bake the scones for about 12 minutes in the top third of the oven until golden brown. Serve lukewarm.

Makes 8 large scones

HOME-MADE GOLDEN SYRUP

For every cup of sugar used, measure a cup of boiling water and a pinch each of cream of tartar and salt.

Melt the sugar in a heavy-based saucepan over low heat and stir constantly until it is a light golden brown. Dissolve the cream of tartar and salt in the boiling water. Add a little at a time to the syrup and boil briskly, uncovered, until a small quantity, quickly chilled in a cold saucer, forms a thick syrup.

FARMER'S DELIGHT

That's the name my husband gives this large scone and he orders it for joyful occasions, such as fountains that start to flow and a farm dam full of water after a good shower of rain on the farm.

275 g cake flour (2 c)
20 ml baking powder (4 t)
2 ml salt (½ t)
80 g butter/margarine (6 T)
1 extra large egg
200 ml milk (¾ c)
60 ml apricot jam (¼ c)

Preheat the oven to 200 °C. Grease a shallow pie dish or pizza plate with a diameter of about 22 cm.

Sift together the cake flour, the baking powder and the salt. Rub 30 ml (2 T) of the butter/margarine into the flour mixture. Beat the egg with the milk. Lightly cut the liquid into the flour mixture with a spatula to form a soft dough.

Spread the dough in the pie dish or pizza plate, using a fork. See that it has a uniform thickness, but the surface should be rough and uneven. Bake the scone for about 20 minutes until golden brown.

Melt the remaining 50 g (4 T) butter/margarine and brush the hot scone with it just after removing it from the oven. Leave to cool for a while.

Warm the apricot jam slightly and trickle it over the lukewarm scone. Serve the scone immediately.

Makes 6–8 servings

STORAGE OF FLOUR

Store it in a clean, dry, airtight container in a cool place. Never add fresh flour to old flour.

Fresh cake flour may be stored at room temperature for up to six months, self-raising flour for up to three months and wholewheat flour must be used within two months.

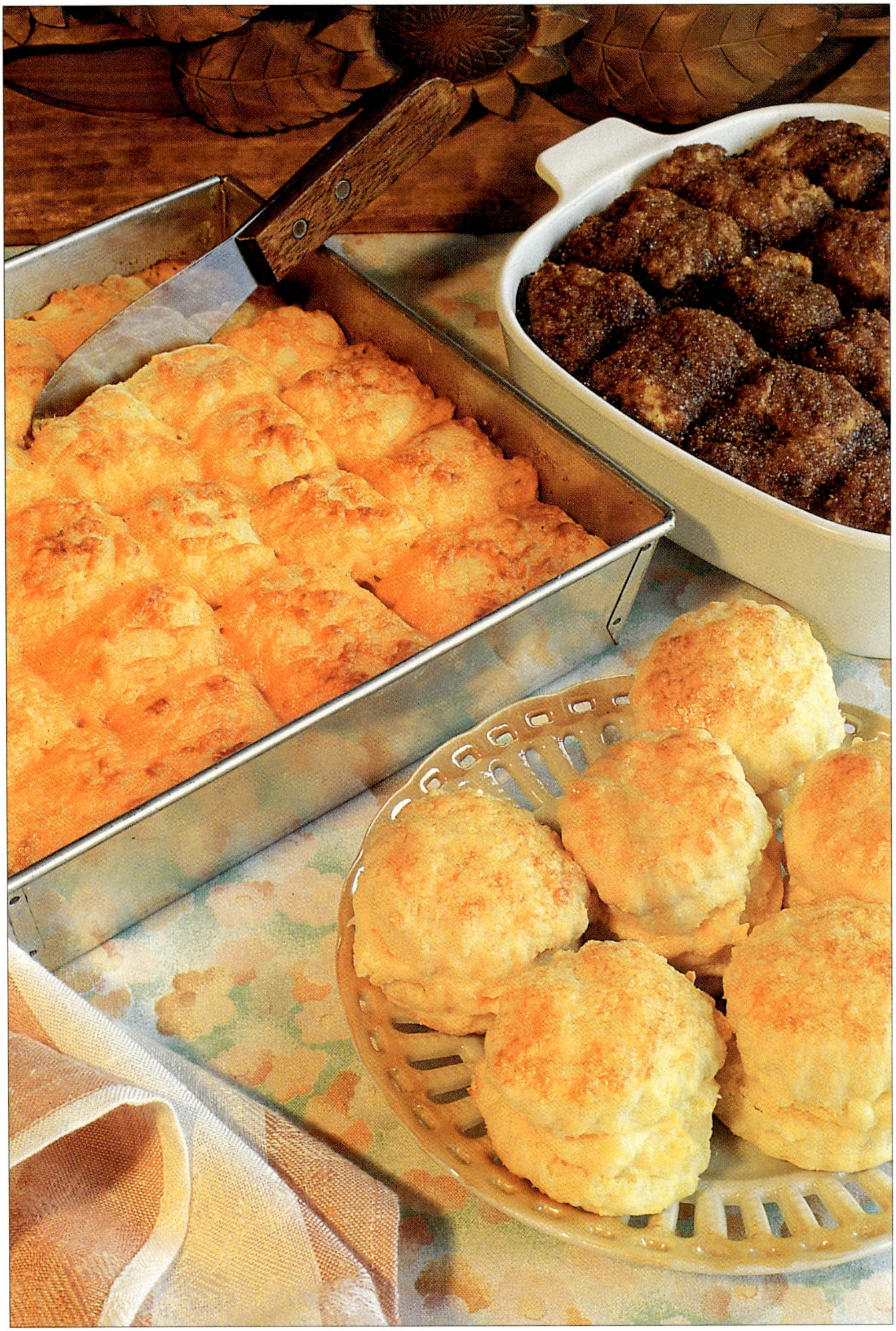

OLD FAITHFUL SCONES

The secret of successful scones is never to stir the liquid into the dry ingredients with a spoon, but to cut it in with a spatula.
For a good colour, brush the raw scones with an egg yolk beaten together with 15 ml (1 T) milk, or with just a little milk.

275 g cake flour (2 c)
15 ml baking powder (1 T)
2 ml salt (½ t)
125 g butter/margarine
125 ml milk (½ c)
1 extra large egg

Preheat the oven to 200 °C. Sift together the cake flour, the baking powder and the salt. Rub the butter/margarine into the flour mixture. Beat the milk with the egg. Cut it into the flour mixture till blended.

Roll out the dough to a thickness of 2 cm on a floured pastry board. Cut out circles, 5 cm in diameter, with a biscuit cutter. Place the circles slightly apart on a greased baking sheet. Bake the scones for about 12 minutes until golden brown on top. Place on a wire rack to cool.

Makes 16 scones

CHEESE FILLING FOR SCONES

Bake 16 ordinary scones according to the recipe for Old Faithful Scones. Halve the scones. Spread the cheese filling thickly on the scones and garnish with shredded biltong, chopped parsley or paprika.

30 ml butter/margarine (2 T)
30 g cake flour (3 T)
2 ml salt (½ t)
pinch of cayenne pepper
250 ml milk (1 c)
100 g coarsely grated Cheddar cheese (1 c)

Melt the butter/margarine. Stir in the cake flour, the salt and the cayenne pepper. Add the milk and beat the white sauce thoroughly to avoid lumps. Bring to the boil and stir at regular intervals. Add half the cheese and stir until the cheese melts. Leave the filling to cool completely, then stir in the remaining cheese.

Makes enough filling for 32 scone halves

TOPPINGS FOR SCONES

Make scone dough according to the recipe for Old Faithful Scones. Press the dough lightly into a greased, ovenproof dish measuring 20 cm x 20 cm. Cut into 5 cm squares. Prepare one of these toppings:

CHEESE TOPPING
125 g butter/margarine
100 g coarsely grated Cheddar cheese (1 c)
5 ml mustard powder (1 t)

CINNAMON SUGAR TOPPING
125 g butter/margarine
100 g soft brown sugar (½ c)
10 ml cinnamon (2 t)

Heat the butter/margarine over low heat until just melted. Add the Cheddar cheese and mustard powder or the brown sugar and cinnamon and mix. Spoon the cheese or cinnamon mixture over the raw dough.

Bake the scones for approximately 20 minutes at 200 °C until golden brown and done. Serve lukewarm.

Makes 16 scones

OAT AND APPLE MUFFINS

These muffins contain pieces of apple and are covered by a wonderful crumbly topping. Eat them while lukewarm: just as they are for breakfast, with cream at teatime or with ice cream for dessert.

    150 g oats (1½ c)
    150 g soft brown sugar (¾ c)
    140 g cake flour (1 c)
    5 ml cinnamon (1 t)
    175 g butter/margarine (¾ c)
    10 ml baking powder (2 t)
    5 ml bicarbonate of soda (1 t)
    5 ml salt (1 t)
    100 g wholewheat flour (¾ c)
    1 tin (385 g) unsweetened pie apples
    125 ml buttermilk (½ c)
    2 extra large eggs

Preheat the oven to 200 °C. Lightly grease 18 muffin cups. Mix a topping of 100 g (1 c) of the oats, 50 g (4 T) of the brown sugar, 40 g (4 T) of the cake flour and the cinnamon. Rub in 50 g (4 T) of the butter/margarine to form a crumbly mixture.

Sift together the remaining 100 g (¾ c) cake flour, the baking powder, bicarbonate of soda and salt. Add the wholewheat flour and the remaining 100 g (½ c) brown sugar and 50 g (½ c) oats and mix.

Chop up the pie apples and stir into the flour mixture. Beat the buttermilk with the eggs. Melt the remaining 125 g butter/margarine and beat it into the egg mixture. Add this mixture to the flour mixture and stir till just blended.

Fill the greased muffin cups two-thirds full of batter. Sprinkle the topping lavishly on top of the batter.

Bake the muffins for about 25 minutes until done and slightly brown on top. Turn out carefully onto a wire rack to cool slightly.

Makes 1½ dozen muffins

DATE MUFFINS

These muffins are moist and pleasantly soft in texture. Eat them just as they are, or cut them open and butter lightly.

For a special occasion, you can add a few roughly chopped pecan nuts or walnuts to the batter towards the end.

```
250 g dates
5 ml bicarbonate of soda (1 t)
375 ml boiling water (1½ c)
125 ml smooth apricot jam (½ c)
100 g soft brown sugar (½ c)
50 g butter/margarine (4 T)
1 extra large egg
275 g cake flour (2 c)
10 ml baking powder (2 t)
1 ml salt (¼ t)
```

Chop up the dates and remove stones if there are any. Sprinkle the bicarbonate of soda over the dates. Pour the boiling water over the mixture and stir well. Allow to cool till lukewarm.

Preheat the oven to 180 °C. Lightly grease 20 muffin cups.

Beat together the apricot jam, brown sugar, butter/margarine and egg until well blended. Stir in the date mixture.

Sift together the cake flour, baking powder and salt. Add it to the date mixture and beat till well mixed.

Fill the muffin cups about three-quarters full of batter. Bake the muffins for about 20 minutes until completely done and slightly brown on top. Leave the muffins to cool in the pans for a few minutes before carefully turning them out on to a wire rack to cool completely.

The muffins freeze well. Place them in a freezer container and interleave them with waxed paper so that they do not stick together when frozen.

Makes 20 muffins

BRAN MUFFINS WITH RAISINS

One of our great breakfast favourites. The muffins are fibre-rich, taste very good with all the raisins and are pleasantly moist. We eat them with butter and marmalade.

    200 g soft brown sugar (1 c)
    125 ml sunflower oil (½ c)
    2 extra large eggs
    5 ml salt (1 t)
    70 g bran (2 c)
    500 ml milk (2 c)
    10 ml bicarbonate of soda (2 t)
    150 g seedless raisins (1 c)
    325 g wholewheat flour (2½ c)

Preheat the oven to 190 °C. Lightly grease 24 muffin cups.

Beat the brown sugar, sunflower oil, eggs and salt very well. Stir in the bran, also the milk in which the bicarbonate of soda has been dissolved, and the raisins. Add the flour and stir till just mixed.

Fill the muffin cups about two-thirds full of batter. Bake the muffins for about 20 minutes until they become slightly browned on top. Turn the muffins out onto a wire rack to cool.

Makes 2 dozen muffins

MARVELLOUS MARMALADE

Make the marmalade from the first ripe fruit of the season, picked fresh from the trees. Use an orange, lemon, grapefruit and enough naartjies to make a combined weight of 1 kg. Wash the fruit and shred finely. Add 3 litres (12 c) water and leave to stand overnight.

Boil the mixture the following morning until the shredded fruit is soft. Add 2,5 kg (12½ c) sugar and boil uncovered for half an hour. Begin to test for the formation of jelly and boil more slowly. When a little cooled marmalade wrinkles if you push it with your finger, it is thick enough.

CHEESE AND CURRANT MUFFINS

The golden rule of successful muffins is to stir the liquid into the dry ingredients until the dry ingredients are just moistened. If you mix the batter too much, the muffins produce so many holes during baking that it looks as though a mole has tried to dig tunnels in them.

   400 g self-raising flour (3 c)
   15 ml baking powder (1 T)
   15 ml sugar (1 T)
   5 ml salt (1 t)
   100 g coarsely grated Cheddar cheese (1 c)
   75 g currants (½ c)
   250 ml buttermilk (1 c)
   125 ml sunflower oil (½ c)
   60 ml milk (¼ c)
   2 extra large eggs

Preheat the oven to 230 °C. Lightly grease 18 muffin cups.

Sift together the self-raising flour, the baking powder, the sugar and the salt. Add the Cheddar cheese and currants and mix together lightly.

Beat together the buttermilk, sunflower oil, milk and eggs. Add this to the flour mixture and stir till just mixed.

Fill the greased muffin cups with batter. Bake the muffins for about 12–15 minutes until they become golden brown on top. Leave them to cool in the pans for a minute or two, then turn them out onto a wire rack to cool a little longer. Serve the muffins lukewarm, with butter.

Makes 18 muffins

VARIATION

The currants may be replaced with the same amount of seedless raisins which have been chopped into smaller pieces.

BREAD AND ROLLS

The aroma of freshly baked bread makes your mouth water and it's very hard to have to wait before eating that first slice – the crust! Fresh bread like this tastes best with only butter on it. The same applies to bread rolls. In summer, there's no better breakfast or supper than a cup of tea with slices of fresh buttered wholewheat bread eaten with chilled figs that have ripened on the trees to the peak of sweetness.

FRENCH BREAD

It's easy to make these loaves yourself – and much more cheaply than the bakery.

1 kg cake flour (7¼ c)
1 packet (10 g) instant dry yeast
15 ml salt (1 T)
15 ml sugar (1 T)
30 ml butter/margarine (2 T)
625 ml warm water (2½ c)
1 egg yolk
15 ml milk (1 T)
sesame seed, linseed or poppy seed

Mix together the cake flour, instant dry yeast, salt and sugar. Melt the butter/margarine in the water. Mix gradually with the flour mixture. Knead the dough well until it is smooth and elastic.

Place the dough in a large, well-oiled mixing bowl. Turn the dough in the bowl so that the oiled side faces upwards. Cover it loosely with plastic and cover the bowl warmly. Leave the dough to rise until it has doubled in volume.

Knock down the dough and divide into thirds. Roll each third into a sausage and place on a large greased baking sheet. Make diagonal cuts on top of each loaf. Beat the egg yolk and milk. Brush the loaves with it and sprinkle with sesame seed, linseed or poppy seed. Cover loosely with plastic and leave the loaves to rise for about 20 minutes at room temperature until doubled in volume.

Preheat the oven to 220 °C. Place a small container of boiling water in the bottom of the oven. Bake the loaves in the middle of the oven for approximately 20 minutes till golden brown.

Makes 3 medium French loaves

GARLIC BREAD

Cut a French loaf into slices, but not right through to the base.

Peel and crush two cloves of garlic. Mix the garlic with 125 g butter/margarine and a little finely grated Cheddar cheese. Add 30 ml (2 T) sherry and a pinch of dried mixed herbs and blend well.

Spread the filling lavishly between the slices of bread. Wrap the loaf in a piece of aluminium foil. Bake for 15–20 minutes at 180 °C until steaming hot.

Cut the slices right through to the base and serve the bread hot.

BREAD AND ROLLS 137

BRAN RAISIN BREAD

On the farm, there's never really very much time for an elaborate breakfast on a Sunday morning. We like to have just a slice or two of this lovely moist bran raisin bread and butter with a cup of tea before we set off for church.

>   500 ml milk (2 c)
>   250 g seedless raisins (1¾ c)
>   150 g sugar (¾ c)
>   80 g All-Bran flakes (2 c)
>   275 g self-raising flour (2 c)
>   5 ml salt (1 t)

Mix the milk, raisins, sugar and bran flakes. Leave to soak overnight.

Preheat the oven to 180 °C. Grease a narrow loaf tin with a volume of 1,5 litres (6 c). Line the tin with waxed paper.

Add the self-raising flour and the salt to the milk mixture and stir until it forms a soft, loose dough. Spoon the dough into the loaf tin and spread evenly.

Bake the bread for 1½ hours. Turn it out onto a wire rack, remove the waxed paper and allow to cool.

Makes a medium loaf

VARIATION

'I have already made this Bran Raisin Bread twice, and it's certainly a big hit in the Coetzee household. The second time, I used only half the raisins and added a handful of sunflower seeds, and it was also very good!' writes Thea Coetzee.

Thea is the editor at Struik Publishers who has to see to it that this book is faultless when it appears in the book shops.

SEED LOAF

Here is an easy recipe for a loaf which not only tastes wonderful, but is also very nutritious. If you have poppy or sesame seed, sprinkle a little over the raw dough before popping the loaf into the oven.

I toast the sunflower seeds before using. Toasted sunflower seeds are not only more palatable, but also don't turn green during the baking process.

Linseed is available at shops that sell health products. It is the seed of flax which when pressed, yields linseed oil.

    260 g wholewheat flour (2 c)
    100 g oats (1 c)
    75 g shelled sunflower seed (½ c)
    40 g All-Bran flakes (1 c)
    40 g linseed (4 T)
    500 ml buttermilk (2 c)
    15 ml sunflower oil (1 T)
    15 ml honey/molasses (1 T)
    7 ml bicarbonate of soda (1½ t)
    5 ml salt (1 t)

Preheat the oven to 180 °C. Grease a loaf tin with a volume of approximately 1,5 litres (6 c).

Mix the wholewheat flour, oats, sunflower seed, bran flakes and linseed. Beat together the buttermilk, sunflower oil, honey/molasses, bicarbonate of soda and salt. Add this to the flour mixture and mix well. Spoon the dough into the loaf tin and spread evenly.

Bake the loaf for about 1¼ hours until completely done. Turn it out onto a wire rack and leave it to cool.

Makes a medium loaf

HINT
The buttermilk may be replaced with unflavoured yoghurt or with 500 ml (2 c) full cream milk to which 37,5 ml (2½ T) lemon juice or vinegar has been added.

BREAD AND ROLLS

CHRIS'S WHEATEN LOAF

'Don't you think that we should have whole grains of wheat in our bread?' Chris asked one day. I modified my old bread recipe slightly and added some soaked pearl wheat. We liked it so much that I now bake it regularly just for the two of us.

 400 g pearl wheat (2 c)
 1 kg wholewheat flour (7½ c)
 1 kg cake flour (7¼ c)
 80 g skim milk powder (¾ c)
 1 packet (10 g) instant dry yeast
 30 ml sugar (2 T)
 30 ml salt (2 T)
 875 ml warm water (3½ c)
 50 ml sunflower oil (3 T)

Cover the pearl wheat with plenty of cold water the previous evening, heat it to boiling point and leave to stand overnight. Bring the soaked pearl wheat to the boil again the next morning, leave to cool until lukewarm and drain very well.

Mix the wholewheat flour, cake flour, milk powder, instant dry yeast, sugar and salt. Add the pearl wheat, warm water and sunflower oil. Knead well until it forms a soft, manageable dough.

Place the dough in a large bowl that has been greased with sunflower oil. Turn the dough in the bowl so that the oiled side faces upwards. Cover it loosely with plastic and cover the bowl warmly. Leave it to rise until it has doubled in volume.

Preheat the oven to 180 °C. Grease four loaf tins, each with a volume of about 1,5 litres (6 c).

Knock down the dough and divide into quarters. Form a loaf from each and place in the tins. Cover loosely with plastic and leave to rise just until the tins are full.

Bake the loaves for 1¼ hours. Turn out and wrap them in a bread cloth.

Makes 4 medium loaves

MEALIE BREAD

This instant bread is made with mealie meal and is traditionally baked for breakfast in the southern states of the USA, where the Americans call it 'Johnny cake' or 'spoon bread'.

My version of this bread contains sweetcorn. I usually brush a little melted butter over the hot crust when I take the bread out of the oven.

The bread tastes best when it is eaten lukewarm. We usually eat it with butter and golden syrup and sometimes with honey, apricot jam or grated cheese.

   200 g cake flour (1½ c)
   200 g sifted mealie meal (1½ c)
   75 g sugar (6 T)
   15 ml baking powder (1 T)
   5 ml salt (1 t)
   75 ml milk (5 T)
   60 ml sunflower oil (¼ c)
   2 extra large eggs
   1 tin (420 g) cream-style sweetcorn

Preheat the oven to 200 °C. Grease a cake tin measuring 20 cm x 20 cm and line the base of the tin with waxed paper.

Sift together the cake flour, mealie meal, sugar, baking powder and salt. Beat together the milk, sunflower oil and eggs. Add the milk mixture and the sweetcorn to the flour mixture and stir till just mixed. Spoon the batter into the greased cake tin and spread it evenly.

Bake the bread for about 35–40 minutes until it is golden brown. Turn it out carefully onto a wire rack and leave to cool for a while. Remove the waxed paper and then cut the bread into squares measuring 5 cm x 5 cm. Handle the bread with care, because it crumbles easily.

Makes 16 squares

BRAAIVLEIS BREAD

When we light the fire in the late afternoon to braai some meat at dusk, I quickly rustle up this delicious loaf and pop it into the oven. By the time the coals are ready for the braai, the bread is ready to be taken from the oven.

The bread has a lovely flavour and it looks most appetizing with its green specks of parsley in dough which is coloured light yellow by the turmeric and cheese.

    500 g self-raising flour
    5 ml salt (1 t)
    2 ml turmeric (½ t)
    pinch of cayenne pepper
    100 g coarsely grated Cheddar cheese (1 c)
    1 packet white onion soup powder
    15 ml dried parsley (1 T)
    5 ml garlic flakes (1 t)
    500 ml buttermilk (2 c)
    125 ml sunflower oil (½ c)
    2 eggs

Preheat the oven to 180 °C. Grease a loaf tin with a volume of 1,5 litres (6 c). Line the tin with waxed paper.

Sift together the self-raising flour, salt, turmeric and cayenne pepper. Add the cheese, white onion soup powder, parsley and garlic flakes and mix.

Beat together the buttermilk, sunflower oil and eggs and mix this with the flour mixture. Place the dough in the tin and spread it evenly.

Bake the loaf for approximately an hour until done and nicely browned on top. Turn it out, remove the waxed paper and leave it to cool for a while.

Eat it lukewarm and lightly buttered.

Makes a medium loaf

POTATO BREAD

This is a quick loaf made with self-raising flour, and it tastes as good as it looks. The potatoes make it pleasantly moist and the herbs give it its characteristic taste. It's perfect for a braai.

To vary the recipe, you may sometimes omit the garlic and replace the rosemary with the same amount of caraway seeds or even aniseed.

> 3 medium potatoes
> 75 ml cream or evaporated milk (5 T)
> 1 extra large egg
> 2 cloves garlic
> 7 ml salt (1½ t)
> 350 g self-raising flour (2½ c)
> 15 ml fresh or dried rosemary (1 T)
> cake flour

Boil the potatoes in their jackets in plenty of water until they are tender. Plunge them into cold water. Remove the skins and press the potatoes through a sieve.

Beat together the cream or evaporated milk and the egg. Peel and crush the cloves of garlic.

Mix the mashed potatoes, egg mixture, garlic and salt. Add the self-raising flour and rosemary and mix well. Shape the dough into a ball. Place it on a baking sheet lined with aluminium foil. Dust the ball of dough with a little cake flour and make shallow cuts in the top of the bread so that when the loaf is baked, it is easy to divide it into portions.

Bake the loaf for approximately an hour at 190 °C until golden brown and done. Place it on a wire rack to cool for a while. Serve it lukewarm.

Makes a medium loaf

WHOLEWHEAT BANANA LOAF

This loaf is splendid for breakfast. It is also excellent for long journeys, the children will love some of it in their lunch tins and it goes down very well at those meetings which require a plate of eats.

The bananas can be overripe, and the buttermilk may be replaced with the same amount of full cream milk to which 30 ml (2 T) vinegar has been added.

200 g cake flour (1½ c)
10 ml baking powder (2 t)
5 ml salt (1 t)
200 g wholewheat flour (1½ c)
150 g soft brown sugar (¾ c)
50 g butter/margarine (4 T)
150 g seedless raisins (1 c)
100 g chopped nuts (1 c)
375 ml buttermilk (1½ c)
1 extra large egg
5 ml bicarbonate of soda (1 t)
2 large ripe bananas

Preheat the oven to 180 °C. Grease a loaf tin with a volume of about 1,5 litres (6 c). Line the tin with waxed paper.

Sift together the cake flour, baking powder and salt. Add the wholewheat flour and brown sugar and mix. Rub the butter/margarine into the flour mixture. Add the raisins and nuts and mix.

Beat together the buttermilk, egg and bicarbonate of soda. Mash the bananas. Add the buttermilk mixture and mashed bananas to the flour mixture and combine well. Spoon the dough into the loaf tin.

Bake the loaf for approximately an hour till done. Turn out onto a wire rack to cool. Remove the waxed paper.

Makes a medium loaf

DATE LOAF

This recipe, which comes from my mother's family, is always in use in my home. If I really want to see my husband happy, I make him this date loaf. I store it in the refrigerator to keep it ice cold. At teatime I slice the chilled loaf and serve it spread with a little butter.

I find that if you leave the dates whole, the sliced loaf looks much more attractive. You could also stir 100 g (1 c) chopped almonds or pecan nuts into the batter.

Date loaf freezes very well.

   250 g dates
   5 ml bicarbonate of soda (1 t)
   250 ml boiling water (1 c)
   115 g butter/margarine (½ c)
   100 g sugar (½ c)
   2 extra large eggs
   5 ml vanilla essence (1 t)
   275 g cake flour (2 c)
   10 ml baking powder (2 t)
   2 ml salt (½ t)

Loosen the dates and remove the stones if there are any. Sprinkle with bicarbonate of soda. Pour the boiling water over the dates. Leave for a while to soften.

Preheat the oven to 180 °C. Grease a loaf tin with a volume of 1,5 litres (6 c). Line the tin with waxed paper.

Cream the butter/margarine and sugar. Beat in the eggs one by one. Stir in the vanilla essence and date mixture.

Sift together the cake flour, baking powder and salt. Stir this into the date mixture. Pour the batter into the loaf tin.

Bake the loaf for about 1¼ hours until done. Turn out onto a wire rack, remove the waxed paper and leave to cool.

Makes a medium loaf

HOLLAND
Vischhoek
BAAY FALSO
(False Bay)
Bluff Point
Hanglip

FRUIT BAPS

One of my most pleasant memories of Scotland is eating freshly baked baps one misty morning in the north at Kyle of Lochalsh, while waiting for the boat to the island of Skye.

By the way, a bap is a soft, oval, white bread roll which is typically Scottish. I add dried fruit, but the traditional Scottish baps don't contain any fruit.

850 g cake flour (6½ c)
1 packet (10 g) instant dry yeast
15 ml castor sugar (1 T)
10 ml salt (2 t)
115 g butter/margarine (½ c)
250 ml milk (1 c)
250 ml water (1 c)
150 g dried fruit cake mix (1 c)

Sift together the cake flour, instant dry yeast, castor sugar and salt. Rub in the butter/margarine.

Heat the milk and water till just warm. Stir the liquid into the flour mixture. Add the dried fruit cake mix. Knead the dough well till soft and pliable.

Place the dough in a large bowl that has been liberally greased with sunflower oil. Turn the dough in the bowl so that the oiled side faces upwards. Cover it with plastic and cover the dish warmly. Let the dough rise till doubled in volume.

Preheat the oven to 200 °C. Grease two large baking sheets.

Divide the dough into 18 equal pieces. Roll each piece into a ball. Flatten each ball with the palm of your hand and, using a rolling pin, roll each ball lightly to form an oval shape. Place them a little distance apart on the baking sheets. Cover them with plastic and leave to rise until doubled in volume.

Brush the risen rolls lightly with a little extra milk. Press a hollow in the middle of each roll with your thumb.

Bake the rolls for about 20 minutes until golden brown and done. Place them on wire racks to cool.

Makes 18 rolls

PITA BREAD

It's fascinating to watch pita bread baking, because right before your eyes, these flat bits of dough puff up so quickly that it seems that they'll take off. Just before serving, fill these pockets of bread with any savoury filling and fresh salad greens.

730 g cake flour (5½ c)
1 packet (10 g) instant dry yeast
10 ml salt (2 t)
5 ml castor sugar (1 t)
450 ml warm water (1¾ c)

Sift together the cake flour, instant dry yeast, salt and castor sugar. Add the water to the flour mixture and mix. Knead well to form a soft, pliable dough.

Divide the dough into 12 equal portions and shape each piece into a ball. Roll out each ball to a thickness of approximately 5 mm on a floured pastry board to form a circle. Place all the circles on a floured surface and cover them with a damp cloth. Leave the dough circles to rise till double the original thickness.

Place a large baking sheet low in the oven. Preheat the oven to 240 °C.

Using an egg slice, carefully place three of the pitas at a time onto the hot, ungreased baking sheet. Bake the pitas for about 4 minutes just until they are completely puffed out.

Makes a dozen pita breads

WHITE BREAD ROLLS

Once, when we were visiting the Oberholsters of Lichtenburg, I was paging through Eloma's cookbook at the kitchen table while she was making our meal. 'You must write down that bread roll recipe. Nobody bakes bread rolls like my aunt Tol of Johannesburg,' she said.

Aunt Tol van der Merwe will surely forgive me for using instant dry yeast when baking her bread rolls, because fresh, compressed yeast is seldom available in our neck of the woods.

I brush the bread rolls with a little milk, sprinkle poppy or sesame seeds on top and cut a cross in each roll with a pair of scissors before leaving them to rise.

> 700 ml milk (2¾ c)
> 30 ml butter/margarine (2 T)
> 30 ml sugar (2 T)
> 1 kg cake flour (7¼ c)
> 1 packet (10 g) instant dry yeast
> 12,5 ml salt (2½ t)

Bring the milk, butter/margarine and sugar to the boil, making sure it doesn't boil over. Cool till lukewarm.

Sift together the cake flour, instant dry yeast and salt. Add this mixture to the milk mixture and knead to form a soft, pliable dough. Place the dough in a large bowl that has been liberally greased with sunflower oil. Turn the dough in the bowl so that the oiled side faces upwards. Cover it with plastic and cover the dish warmly. Leave the dough to rise until it has doubled in volume.

Preheat the oven to 200 °C. Grease two large baking sheets.

Shape bread rolls from the dough and place them slightly apart on the baking sheets. Cover them loosely with plastic and leave to rise until doubled in volume. Bake the rolls for about 20 minutes until done and light brown on top.

Makes approximately 30 rolls

CRESCENT ROLLS

When we have guests at our breakfast table, they are usually most impressed when they hear that I bake these beautiful rolls myself. Little do they know how easy it is! The rolls look quite impressive and they also freeze very well.

- 540 g cake flour (4 c)
- 30 ml baking powder (2 T)
- 5 ml salt (1 t)
- pinch of cayenne pepper
- 125 g butter/margarine
- 200 g coarsely grated Cheddar cheese (2 c)
- 375 ml milk (1½ c)
- 1 egg

Preheat the oven to 200 °C. Place the oven rack in the top third of the oven. Line a baking sheet with aluminium foil.

Sift together the cake flour, baking powder, salt and cayenne pepper. Rub in the butter/margarine until the mixture resembles mealie meal. Add the Cheddar cheese and mix. Using a spatula, cut the milk into the flour mixture a little at a time to form a dough.

Flour a pastry board and rolling pin. Divide the dough into quarters. Roll each quarter into a circle with a thickness of about 7 mm and a diameter of 22 cm. Cut the circle into eighths like the spokes of a wheel. Roll up each wedge from the outer edge to the tip. Bend the rolls into the shape of crescents. Place them slightly apart on the baking sheet.

Beat the egg and brush the rolls with it. Bake them for about 15 minutes until golden brown on top. Place on a wire rack and leave to cool.

Makes 32 rolls

COUNTRY ROLLS

I always have some of these wholewheat rolls in the freezer, because when my husband needs something to eat when going on a journey, these bread rolls with cheese and lettuce or cucumber slices are much better than ordinary sandwiches.

   1 kg cake flour (7¼ c)
   200 g wholewheat flour (1½ c)
   1 packet (10 g) instant dry yeast
   30 ml sugar (2 T)
   7 ml salt (1½ t)
   2 extra large eggs
   500 ml milk (2 c)
   375 ml boiling water (1½ c)
   125 ml sunflower oil (½ c)
   sesame or poppy seed

Mix the cake flour, wholewheat flour, instant dry yeast, sugar and salt. Beat the eggs and reserve 30 ml (2 T) for brushing the rolls. Beat the rest with the milk, the boiling water and the sunflower oil until just mixed. Add the milk mixture to the flour mixture and combine. Knead well to make a smooth, soft dough.

Place the dough in a large bowl greased with a little sunflower oil. Turn the dough in the bowl so that the oiled side faces upwards. Cover the dough and place it in a warm place. Leave it to rise until it has doubled in volume.

Knock down the dough, pinch off balls of dough between the thumb and index finger and place them slightly apart on lightly greased baking sheets. Brush with the reserved beaten egg and sprinkle with sesame or poppy seed. Cut the top of each roll with a pair of scissors. Leave to rise until almost doubled in volume.

Bake the rolls for about 25 minutes in an oven preheated to 200 °C until they are golden brown on top. Place on a wire rack and leave to cool.

Makes about 2½ dozen rolls

WHOLEWHEAT FINGERS

Wholewheat fingers taste very good with braaivleis or soup. When I feel like a cheesy taste, I add a little finely grated Parmesan cheese to the dry ingredients. The dried herbs may be replaced with finely chopped fresh herbs.

125 g butter/margarine
70 g cake flour (½ c)
20 ml baking powder (4 t)
5 ml salt (1 t)
260 g wholewheat flour (2 c)
2 ml dried mixed herbs (½ t)
250 ml milk (1 c)
1 extra large egg

Preheat the oven to 190 °C. Melt the butter/margarine in a shallow, ovenproof dish measuring 35 cm x 23 cm x 5 cm in the oven and remove when melted.

Sift together the cake flour, baking powder and salt. Add the wholewheat flour and herbs and mix.

Beat together the milk and the egg. Cut the milk mixture into the flour mixture with a spatula to form a dough.

Shape the dough into a long sausage on a floured pastry board. Cut the sausage into 24 equally thick portions. Roll each piece into the shape of a finger.

Place the fingers one at a time into the melted butter/margarine in the dish and turn each one so that it is well coated in the butter/margarine.

Bake the fingers for about 15 minutes until golden brown on top. Turn them over carefully and bake for about another 7 minutes until nicely browned on top. Serve them immediately.

Makes 2 dozen fingers

RUSKS

Nowadays, rusks are appearing in so many different guises that you don't always know which recipe to try next. You seldom see old-fashioned rusks being baked any more, because who can resist recipes where you make up your own muesli to use in the rusks, or where you moisten the dough with orange juice rather than with the buttermilk that you have become accustomed to using?

MUESLI RUSKS

You can use 700 g bought muesli for these rusks, but it's much cheaper and also much tastier to make it yourself. The coarsely chopped nuts in the muesli not only give a lovely flavour to these rusks, but also provide texture.

The muesli on its own is a delicious and healthy breakfast mixture – it is certainly a sure-fire cure for constipation! When we have it for breakfast, I add a little chopped dried fruit to the mixture and serve it with either yoghurt or milk.

MUESLI
200 g oats (2 c)
200 g coarsely chopped nuts (2 c)
75 g crumbled Weet-Bix biscuits (1 c)
40 g coconut (½ c)
30 g bran (1 c)
125 ml sunflower oil (½ c)
125 ml honey (½ c)

RUSK DOUGH
700 g butter/margarine (3 c)
500 g sugar (2½ c)
750 ml buttermilk (3 c)
4 extra large eggs
1,5 kg self-raising flour
40 g baking powder (3 T)
7 ml salt (1½ t)

Mix the oats, nuts, Weet-Bix crumbs, coconut and bran. Add the sunflower oil and honey and mix well. Spread open the mixture in a large baking tray. Bake for about 15–20 minutes at 180 °C until it begins to brown. Stir occasionally.

Heat the butter/margarine and sugar until the shortening has melted. Remove from the stove. Beat together the buttermilk and the eggs and stir the buttermilk mixture into the sugar mixture.

Sift together the self-raising flour, the baking powder and the salt. Add the muesli and mix. Add this to the sugar mixture and combine well.

Spoon the dough into four greased loaf tins, each with a volume of 1,5 litres (6 c). Bake the rusk loaves for about 30 minutes at 180 °C and then for about 40 minutes at 160 °C until golden brown and done. Leave the loaves to cool in the tins for a few minutes, then turn them out onto a wire rack to cool completely.

Cut each loaf into rusk-sized portions. Dry out overnight in a cool oven with the oven door slightly ajar.

Makes 700 g (6 c) muesli and about 10½ dozen rusks

RUSKS 153

WHOLEWHEAT JAM RUSKS

Leo and Katryn, our two German shepherd dogs, like these rusks even more than Chris and I do. They know exactly when it's time for coffee and rusks in the afternoon, when they claim their treat of the day. If I dawdle over making the coffee, they soon come to remind me to get a move on.

    500 g butter/margarine
    300 g sugar (1½ c)
    125 ml smooth apricot jam (½ c)
    60 ml sunflower oil (¼ c)
    2 extra large eggs
    500 ml buttermilk (2 c)
    500 g self-raising flour (3½ c)
    30 ml baking powder (2 T)
    7 ml salt (1½ t)
    850 g wholewheat flour (6½ c)
    80 g coconut (1 c)

Line a large Swiss roll tin measuring about 45 cm x 30 cm x 3 cm, with aluminium foil and grease the foil.

Heat the butter/margarine, sugar, jam and sunflower oil in a heavy-based saucepan over low heat until the shortening has just melted. Stir occasionally.

Beat the eggs with a little of the buttermilk. Stir the remaining buttermilk into the butter/margarine mixture. Add the egg mixture and mix well.

Sift the self-raising flour, baking powder and the salt. Add the wholewheat flour and coconut and mix. Combine the flour mixture with the buttermilk mixture.

Spoon the dough into the tin. Press it down evenly with a fork. Mark rectangles of 5 cm x 2,5 cm with an egg slice.

Bake the rusks for 15 minutes at 180 °C and then for about 20 minutes at 160 °C until done and browned on top.

Turn out the rusks onto a wire rack and remove the aluminium foil. Leave to cool slightly. Break into rectangles with a fork. Dry out overnight in a cool oven with the oven door slightly ajar.

Makes 9 dozen rusks

MILK RUSKS

They look a lot like yeast rusks and taste a lot like buttermilk rusks.

When I dry out the fresh rusks, I place them on wire racks in two large baking trays in the oven. The crumbs then fall neatly into the baking trays and not on the floor of the oven.

> 750 ml milk (3 c)
> 300 g sugar (1½ c)
> 250 g butter/margarine
> 10 ml salt (2 t)
> 2 extra large eggs
> 50 ml sunflower oil (3 T)
> 1,6 kg self-raising flour (12 c)
> 12,5 ml cream of tartar (2½ t)

Preheat the oven to 180 °C. Grease a few loaf tins very well.

Heat together the milk, sugar, butter/margarine and salt until the shortening has melted. Leave to cool until lukewarm. Beat together the eggs and the sunflower oil and stir this into the milk mixture. Sift together the self-raising flour and the cream of tartar and mix the flour mixture with the milk mixture. Knead the dough for approximately 8 minutes. (Add a little extra self-raising flour if the dough is unmanageably soft.)

Grease your hands with melted butter/margarine. Using thumb and index finger, pinch off egg-sized balls of dough. Pack them tightly together in the tins.

Bake the rusks for about 45 minutes until they are golden brown and done. Turn out onto a wire rack to cool.

Separate the rusks and halve each one with a fork. Dry out overnight in a cool oven with the oven door slightly ajar.

Makes 8 dozen rusks

ORANGE RUSKS

As the secretary of our local district agricultural union, I see to it that the farmers have something to nibble on at teatime during meetings. When I brought orange rusks, all the men enjoyed them so much that they ate them just dry.

This recipe comes from my mother-in-law. When she entered it in a cooking competition, she won a microwave oven.

My mother-in-law sometimes adds a few bleached sultanas to the raw dough, but you need to be extra careful when drying the rusks that the oven is not too hot, or the fruit will become too dark.

1,5 kg self-raising flour
400 g sugar (2 c)
7 ml baking powder (1½ t)
5 ml salt (1 t)
500 g butter/margarine
finely grated rind of 1 orange
625 ml orange juice (2½ c)
2 extra large eggs

Preheat the oven to 180 °C. Grease three medium loaf tins.

Sift the self-raising flour, sugar, baking powder and salt. Rub the butter/margarine and orange rind into the mixture until it resembles coarse mealie meal.

Beat together the orange juice and eggs. Mix this with the flour mixture.

Shape the dough between the palms of your hands into egg-sized little balls and pack them tightly together in the loaf tins. Bake the rusks for about 50 minutes until done and light brown on top. Turn out onto a wire rack and leave to cool.

Separate the rusks and halve each rusk with a fork. Pack onto wire racks and dry out overnight in a cool oven with the oven door slightly ajar.

Makes about 9 dozen rusks

SPOON RUSKS

These rusks have absolutely no frills. They are just ordinary, delicious, white buttermilk rusks, which are quickly mixed and even more quickly dished into the pans – with a spoon!

    500 g butter/margarine
    300 g sugar (1½ c)
    750 ml buttermilk (3 c)
    4 extra large eggs
    7 ml salt (1½ t)
    1,5 kg self-raising flour

Cut the butter/margarine into pieces and place in a large heavy-based saucepan. Add the sugar. Warm this mixture over low heat until the butter/margarine has melted. Stir the mixture occasionally.

Add the buttermilk and stir over low heat until the sugar has dissolved. Cool the mixture until it is lukewarm.

Meanwhile grease three to four medium loaf tins. Preheat the oven to 180 °C.

Beat the eggs with the salt and mix this with the lukewarm buttermilk mixture. Add the self-raising flour and mix.

Spoon dessertspoons of the rusk dough (about as large as eggs) into the loaf tins. Dip the spoon in a little sunflower oil after each spoonful.

Bake the rusks for 20 minutes at 180 °C and then for about 30 minutes at 160 °C until done and light brown on top.

Turn the rusks out of the tins. Leave to cool on a wire rack. Separate them and then halve each rusk with a fork.

Pack the rusks onto wire racks and leave to dry out overnight in a cool oven with the oven door slightly ajar.

Makes about 10 dozen rusks

INDEX

A
Almond cake 101
Apple
  bread pudding 79
  dumplings, baked 79
  muffins, oat and 132
  pie, Rosie's 89
Apricot jam, exceptional 124
Aunt Clasina's cup cakes 109
Avocado cream, fish with 41

B
Baby's bean pot 53
Bake
  Green bean 18
  Hake 42
  Helen's chicken and
    vegetable 63
Baked
  apple dumplings 79
  cabbage 24
  maranka in batter 21
  sago pudding 76
Banana
  loaf, wholewheat 144
  pudding 84
Baps, fruit 147
Barbecue seasoning sauce 50
Bars, date 113
Batter crust, vegetable pie
  with 26
Bean(s)
  Bottled green 18
  pot, Baby's 53
  salad, Mother-in-law's 34
  soup with buttermilk
    dumplings 13
Beef, corned 55
Beetroot salad with mayonnaise,
  mixed 33
Biscuits
  Custard 115
  Ginger 112
  Jacoba's crispy 119
  Sielie's spice 117
Bobotie 60
  Pilchard 46
Boerewors 59
  pies 59
Bottled green beans 18
Braaivleis bread 142

Bran
  muffins with raisins 134
  raisin bread 138
Brandy tart, Cape 91
Bread
  Braaivleis 142
  Bran raisin 138
  French 136
  Fried 8
  Garlic 136
  Mealie 141
  Pita 147
  Potato 143
  pudding, apple 79
  pudding, toffee 75
  rolls, white 148
Buttermilk
  chocolate cake 96
  dumplings, bean soup with 13
Butternut soup 15

C
Cabbage
  Baked 24
  Curried 28
  salad, fridge 36
Cake
  Almond 101
  Buttermilk chocolate 96
  Coconut layer 98
  Nut and sultana ring 104
  Orange layer 99
  Short and sweet fruit 105
Cape brandy tart 91
Caramel
  cottage cheese ice cream 85
  tart 94
Carrots
  Curried 28
  with orange sauce 20
Casserole, Creole chicken 62
Cauliflower in blankets 25
Cheese
  and currant muffins 135
  filling for scones 131
Cheesecake 93
  Jonkershoek 100
Chicken
  and vegetable bake,
    Helen's 63
  casserole, Creole 62

  Marinated 65
  Oven-fried 64
  portions, fried 64
Chiffon tart, lemon 92
Chocolate
  cake, buttermilk 96
  delight 83
  shortcake, iced 120
Chris's wheaten loaf 140
Clasina's cup cakes, aunt 109
Coals, veal rib over the 51
Coconut
  layer cake 98
  tart, Greek 90
  tarts, practical 90
Coleslaw dressing 36
Corned beef 55
Cottage cheese ice cream,
  caramel 85
Country rolls 150
Creams, lemon 115
Creole chicken casserole 62
Crescent rolls 149
Crescents 121
Crispy biscuits, Jacoba's 119
Crunchies 118
Cucumbers, sweet and sour 37
Cup cakes, Aunt Clasina's 109
Currant muffins, cheese and 135
Curried
  cabbage 28
  carrots 28
  eggs 71
  rice 22
Curry vetkoek, deep-fried 122
Custard
  biscuits 115
  melkkos 17

D
Date
  bars 113
  loaf 145
  muffins 133
Deep-fried curry vetkoek 122
Doughnuts, quick 108
Dressing, coleslaw 36
Dumplings
  Baked apple 79
  Buttermilk, bean soup with 13
  Rice 77

E
Easy milk tart 88
Eggs, curried 71
Exceptional apricot jam 124

F
Farmer's delight 129
Festival meringue 81
Fibre-rich fish cakes 47
Filled meat roll 56
Filling, pancakes with
  rhubarb 72
Fish
  cakes, fibre-rich 47
  cakes, quick sauce for 47
  Haddock parcels 43
  Hake bake 42
  Litchi 40
  with avocado cream 41
  with pineapple sauce 38
Freckles 111
Freezer meat patties 61
French bread 136
Fridge cabbage salad 36
Fried
  bread 8
  chicken portions 64
  chicken, oven- 64
  curry vetkoek, deep- 122
Frikkadels, tomato 57
Fritters, spinach 23
Fruit
  baps 147
  cake, short and sweet 105
  pudding, steamed 80
  squares 110
  vetkoek 125
Frying pan scone 127

G
Garlic
  bread 136
  kebabs 48
Ginger
  biscuits 112
  tart 95
Golden syrup, home-
  made 128
Gravy powder, savoury 50
Greek coconut tart 90
Green bean(s)
  bake 18
  Bottled 18
Green pea pie, quick 27
Griddle scones, potato 126

H
Haddock parcels 43
Hake bake 42
Hamburger sauce,
  scrumptious 61
Health soup, quick 10
Helen's chicken and vegetable
  bake 63
Home-made golden syrup 128
Hot
  potato salad 32
  rice salad 30
  teacake 102

I
Ice cream
  Caramel cottage cheese 85
  Simple vanilla 85
Iced chocolate shortcake 120
Instant vetkoek 125

J
Jacoba's crispy biscuits 119
Jam
  Exceptional apricot 120
  rusks, wholewheat 154
  slices 116
Jewish tart 86
Jonkershoek cheesecake 100

K
Kebabs, garlic 48
Koeksisters 106

L
Layer
  cake, coconut 98
  cake, orange 99
  pudding, luscious 82
Lemon
  chiffon tart 92
  creams 115
Litchi fish 40
Loaf
  Chris's wheaten 140
  Date 145
  Seed 139
  Wholewheat banana 144

M
Macaroni
  cheese, Monday 69

  Martjie's 68
Maranka in batter, baked 21
Marinated chicken 65
Marmalade, marvellous 134
Martjie's macaroni 68
Marvellous marmalade 134
Mealie bread 141
Meat
  patties, freezer 61
  roll, filled 56
Melkkos, custard 17
Melksnysels 16
Meringue, festival 81
Milk
  noodles 16
  rusks 155
  tart, easy 88
Mixed beetroot salad with
  mayonnaise 33
Monday macaroni cheese 69
Mother-in-law's bean salad 34
Muesli rusks 152
Muffins
  Bran, with raisins 134
  Cheese and currant 135
  Date 133
  Oat and apple 132
Mushroom soup 14

N
Noodle salad 35
Noodles, milk 16
Nourishing vegetable soup 8
Nut and sultana ring cake 104

O
Oat and apple muffins 132
Old faithful scones 131
Orange
  layer cake 99
  pudding 74
  rusks 156
  sauce, carrots with 20
  scones 128
Oven-fried chicken 64
Ox-tongue in tomato and
  mushroom sauce 54

P
Pancakes with rhubarb filling 72
Parcels, haddock 43
Patties, freezer meat 61
Pearl wheat salad 31
Pepper sauce, T-bones with 52

Pie(s)
   Boerewors 59
   Quick green pea 27
   Rosie's apple 89
   Tuna 45
   Vegetable, with batter crust 26
Pilchard bobotie 46
Pineapple sauce, fish with 38
Piquant potato dish 48
Pita bread 147
Pizza, wholewheat 70
Potato
   bread 143
   dish, piquant 48
   griddle scones 126
   salad, hot 32
   soup 11
Pudding
   Apple bread 79
   Baked sago 76
   Banana 84
   Luscious layer 82
   Orange 74
   Steamed fruit 80
   Toffee bread 75

Q
Quick
   doughnuts 108
   green pea pie 27
   health soup 10
   sauce for fish cakes 47

R
Raisin(s)
   Bran muffins with 134
   bread, bran 138
Rhubarb filling, pancakes with 72
Rib, veal over the coals 51
Rice
   Curried 22
   dumplings 77
   salad, hot 30
Ring cake, nut and sultana 104
Roll
   Filled meat 56
   Swiss 103
Rolls
   country 150
   crescent 149
   white bread 148
Rosie's apple pie 89

Rusks
   Milk 155
   Muesli 152
   Orange 156
   Spoon 157
   Wholewheat jam 154

S
Sago pudding, baked 76
Salad
   dressing, coleslaw 36
   Fridge cabbage 36
   Hot potato 32
   Hot rice 30
   Mixed beetroot, with mayonnaise 33
   Noodle 35
   Pearl wheat 31
   Tasty tomato 69
Sauce
   Barbecue seasoning 50
   Carrots with orange 20
   Fish with pineapple 38
   for fish cakes, quick 47
   Ox-tongue in tomato and mushroom 54
   Scrumptious hamburger 61
   T-bones with pepper 52
Savoury
   gravy powder 50
   tart 66
Scone(s)
   Cheese filling for 131
   Frying pan 127
   Old faithful 131
   Orange 128
   Potato griddle 126
   Toppings for 131
Scrumptious hamburger sauce 61
Seasoning sauce, barbecue 50
Seed loaf 139
Short and sweet fruit cake 105
Shortcake, iced chocolate 120
Sielie's spice biscuits 117
Simple vanilla ice cream 85
Snoek tart 45
Soup
   Bean, with buttermilk dumplings 13
   Butternut 15
   Mushroom 14
   Nourishing vegetable 8
   Potato 11
   Quick health 10
Sousboontjies 34

Spice biscuits, Sielie's 117
Spinach fritters 23
Spoon rusks 157
Steamed fruit pudding 80
Sultana ring cake, nut and 104
Sweet and sour cucumbers 37
Sweetcorn vetkoek 124
Swiss roll 103

T
T-bones with pepper sauce 52
Tart
   Cape brandy 91
   Caramel 94
   Easy milk 88
   Ginger 95
   Greek coconut 90
   Jewish 86
   Lemon chiffon 92
   Savoury 66
   Snoek 45
Teacake, hot 102
Toffee bread pudding 75
Tomato
   and mushroom sauce, ox-tongue in 54
   frikkadels 57
   salad, tasty 69
Tongue, ox- in tomato and mushroom sauce 54
Toppings for scones 131
Tuna pie 45

V
Vanilla ice cream, simple 85
Veal rib over the coals 51
Vegetable
   bake, Helen's chicken and 63
   pie with batter crust 26
   soup, nourishing 8
Vetkoek
   Deep-fried curry 122
   Fruit 125
   Instant 125
   Sweetcorn 124

W
Wheat salad, pearl 31
Wheaten loaf, Chris's 140
White bread rolls 148
Wholewheat
   banana loaf 144
   fingers 151
   jam rusks 154
   pizza 70